UNACCOMPANIED

STORIES OF BRAVE TEENAGERS SEEKING ASYLUM

BY

TRACY WHITE

STREET NOISE BOOKS • BROOKLYN, NEW YORK

ISBN 978-1951-491-20-8

Design and production assistance from Dev Kamath
Cover design by Zoe Norvell

Printed in the United States

9 8 7 6 5 4 3 2 1

First Edition

Table of Contents

WARNING: This book contains references to potentially sensitive/upsetting content.

Introduction

Most of my working life has been centered on advocating for teens by creating documentary-style comics, teaching visual storytelling in schools and universities, and leading comic workshops for students from middle school to adults. Authentic teen lives are rarely depicted in media; showing what's real provides connection with others and validation for one's own life.

In 2016, as US border tensions increased, it was the images of young people and teens that went straight to my heart.

But the majority of what they encountered in their lives, good and bad, wasn't talked about. We were only shown the occasional moments of reductive sadness or pain in a photograph.

When I saw those dehumanizing images at the border, I kept asking myself questions about what I didn't see. Who are these incredibly strong, tenacious, brave children? What did they leave behind and why? Who were their friends at home? What do they like to do? What do they think about? Laugh about? My own children range in ages from seven to fourteen. I am very aware of this time in life and how rich their inner lives are.

Eventually my questions led me, through a friend, to the Safe Passage Project. The Safe Passage Project is an organization that provides pro bono legal services to immigrants and refugee children facing deportation.

In the summer of 2018, I accompanied two of their lawyers to the immigration court at Federal Plaza in New York City.

That day I saw the US immigration system in action from the back of a crowded windowless courtroom. On one side, seated behind a long rectangular table, was a government lawyer next to stacks of paper. On the other side, a child who didn't speak English sat next to an interpreter with no legal representation, an empty rectangular table in front of them. This scenario was repeated throughout the day with little variation.

All I wanted to do was something, anything, but I'm not a lawyer, and I don't speak Spanish. I teach and make comics about real-life issues for teens. So I asked the lawyers if a comic would be helpful. The answer, after some discussion and thought, was yes. A bilingual comic explaining the legal system for their clients and the adults in their lives that they could leave in the courthouse, share with sister organizations, and distribute digitally would help a lot.

I began interviewing the legal teams at the Safe Passage Project about the concepts they felt were most important for the comic to contain. Having made a previous documentary comic about young refugee teens and their families for the Lower East Side Tenement Museum, I had a very basic understanding of what life for recent immigrant teens in an immigrant household where they were the primary English speakers was like. But I knew nothing about undergoing the journey to the United States alone or the legal ramifications.

As I was working, I realized that while we were providing very specific help to the teens traversing the US immigration system, the general theme of them as victims was still prevalent in our media.

Narrative has power to challenge beliefs.

People are so much more than the snapshot of pain we are so often shown. Refugees are not passive, needful victims—they all have strength to make life-saving choices.

To have any chance of righting these wrongs and undoing the damage reductive words like *aliens* and *illegals* do to the humanity of a person, I felt there needed to be a book with other viewpoints, alternative language, and broader accounts. To create an inclusive authentic picture, we have to open the research lens as wide as possible in an attempt to understand the magnitude of the choices being made.

In the fall of 2019 I finished the script for the Safe Passage Project and started working on what would eventually become this book.

Over the next year I did more interviews and wrote a script with initial sketchy thumbnails. I thought I was almost done but as I worked, I kept asking myself questions about what I didn't know, realizing that interviews provided a framework, but to really honor these journeys I needed more accountability.

So the research lens widened to include the support and guidance of many people across the globe. I went south of the border and I also scoured the internet to gather reference photos and read US government sites and scholarly papers; followed links to names and contact information; read books on the history and culture of the countries I was writing about; found contemporary playlists and YouTube videos from each country; watched films made in each country; and kept reaching out to anyone who might be willing to shine more light on these accounts by sharing their lived experience or expert knowledge. As a documenter it is my responsibility to constantly check in, ask, listen, and learn.

All events are factual, and while no one has lived the exact lives depicted in the pages, the lives in these pages are founded on truth. The events that occurred were gathered through interviews with lawyers who are immigration/migration/refugee experts. All visuals and conversations have been cross-referenced by people from the countries that each story originated from. And all content has been reviewed by a diversity, equity, and inclusion sensitivity reader.

If we pause, ask, look, listen, and check in we will start to see a whole picture of someone, not just the hurt.

The author's proceeds from the sale of this book will be donated to organizations that support unaccompanied refugee minors and immigrants. If you'd like to donate to any of the incredible places that directly helped in the making of this book, go to www.traced.com/unaccompanied.

If you know of other organizations working to support teen refugees in the United States, please share the knowledge and make the list more comprehensive at www.traced.com/unaccompanied.

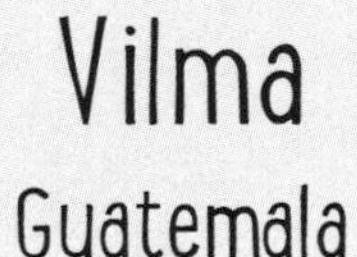

Work hard and tomorrow you will reap what you sow. —Guatemalan proverb

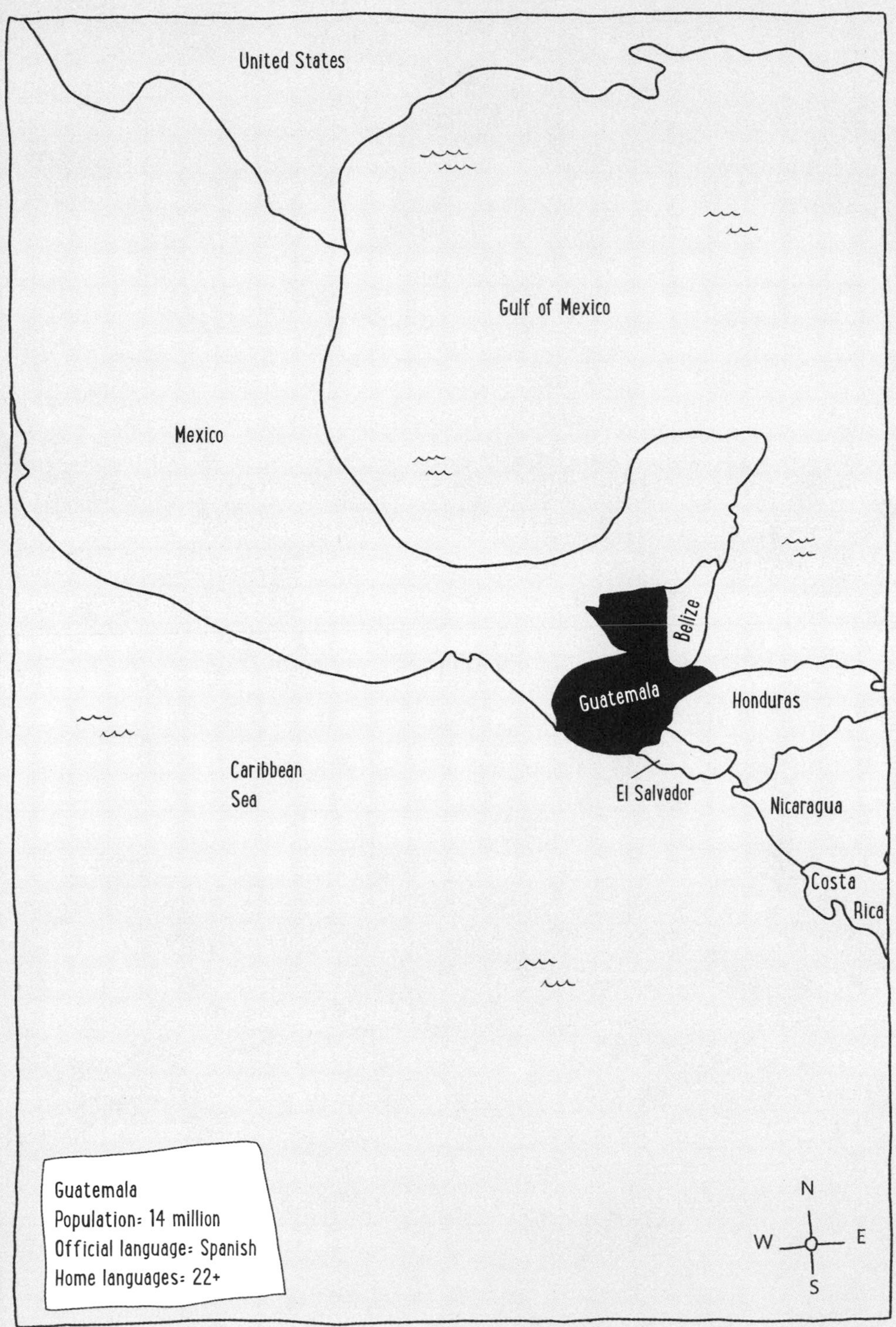
United States
Gulf of Mexico
Mexico
Belize
Guatemala
Honduras
Caribbean Sea
El Salvador
Nicaragua
Costa Rica
Guatemala
Population: 14 million
Official language: Spanish
Home languages: 22+
N
W
E
S

Chicago, 2019

Guatemala, 2017

Papa was unpredictable. Jealous. Anything could set him off.

They lived in a small village between two mountains.

Vilma's dad didn't like her out of his sight.
Come home right after school.

But she found a way to escape.

LET'S GO. VILMA. NOW!

HATE HIM.CAN'T TRUST HIM.LOVE HIM.HAT
HIM.CAN'T TRUST HIM.LOVE HIM.HATE HIM
CAN'TTRUSTHIM.LOVEHIM.HATEHIM.CAN'T
TRUSTHIM.LOVEHIM.HATEHIM.CAN'T TRUST
HIM.LOVEHIM.HATEHIM.CAN'TTRUST HIM.
LOVEHIM.HATEHIM.CAN'TRUSTHIIM.LOVE
HIM.HATEHIM.CAN'TTRUSTHIM.HATEHIM.L
OVEHIM.CAN'TTRUSTHIM.HATEHIM.LOVE H
IM.CAN'TTRUSTHIM.HATEHIM.LOVEHIM.CA
N'TTRUSTHIM.L HATEHIM.CAN'TTR
USTHIM.LOVEH IM.CAN'TTRUSTH
IM.LOVEHIM> 'TTRUSTHIM.L
OVEHIM.HATE RUSTHIM.LOVE
HIM.HATEHI IM.LOVEHIM.H
ATEHIM.CAN EHIM.HATEHI

Vilma had started helping her father in the fields when she was seven*. By the time she was ten, it was routine for her to deal with beatings, work, and school.

*In 2019 over 250,000 Guatemalan children were forced to work, most in agriculture.

And then one day the pattern changed.

STOP!

Papa, STOP!

Please...

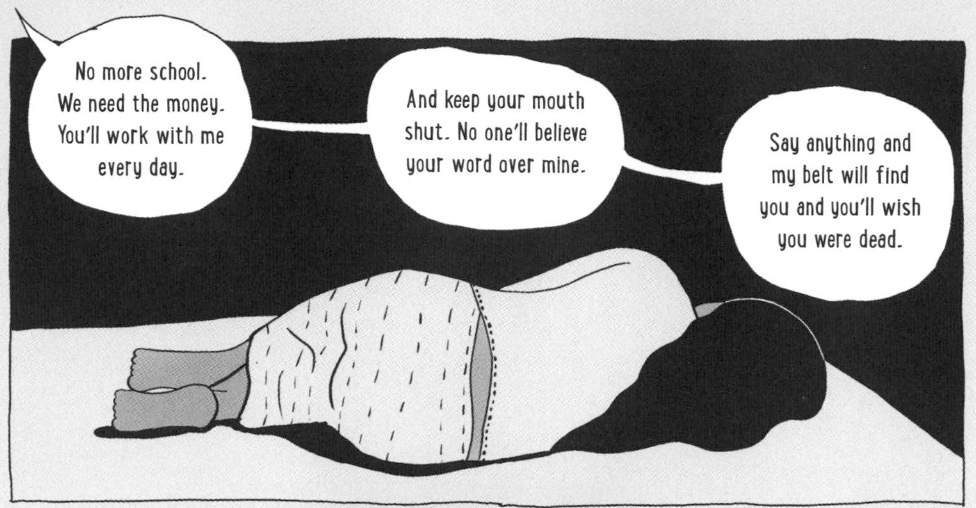
No more school.
We need the money.
You'll work with me
every day.
And keep your mouth
shut. No one'll believe
your word over mine.
Say anything and
my belt will find
you and you'll wish
you were dead.

If I work hard,
maybe he won't
touch me. He
didn't mean to do
this.

But most of the abuse took place in the fields.
Back to
work, Vilma.
Now!

2018, Vilma is thirteen.

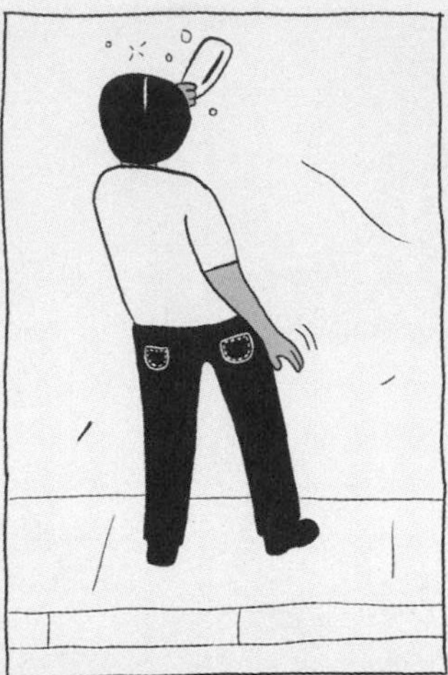

Vilma was alone when Papa came home. Things got more violent than usual.

VILMA!

Be a good girl...
I'LL KILL YOU, YOU WITCH...
DON'T YOU RUN AWAY FROM ME, YOU SHIT!
VILMA. GET BACK HERE!!!!!

What if she doesn't believe me? I'm so bad. This is my fault.

*Guatemalan law favors men in most matters.

Vilma, her sister, and her mom fled to her grandmother's.

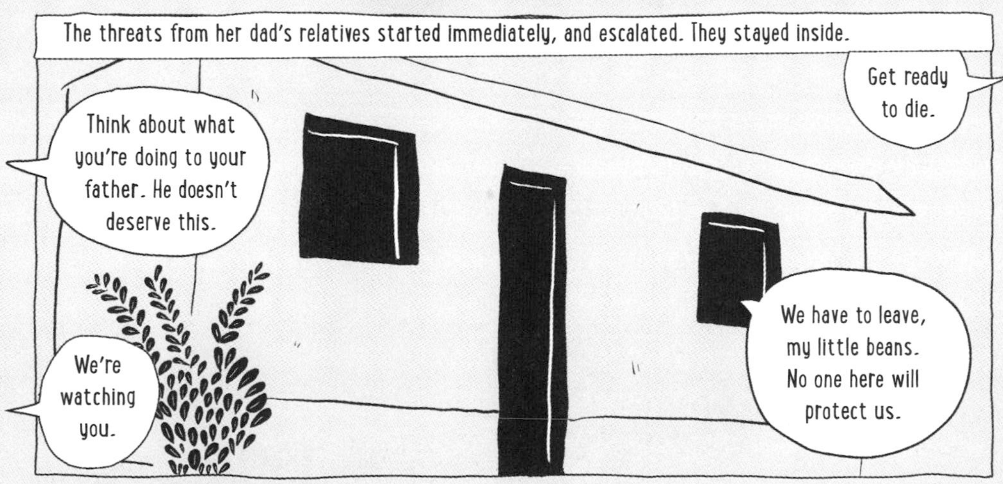

They left that night.

*Mythical white dog protector of travelers and good people.

El Cadejo Blanco will protect us.
What am I forgetting?
If I wasn't here they could stay.

Please, God.
We are in
your hands.
My fault.
My fault.
My fault.
El
Cadejo?

The plan was to take buses and walk to Tijuana, a border city between Mexico and San Diego, California. It would be a longer route but it avoids the drug cartels in Tamaulipas, Mexico. It can be easier to travel unnoticed in small groups. Large caravans attract attention.

As soon as we're in Mexico I'll change our quetzales to pesos.

Money's divided between us to keep it safe.

What else? What else?

God willing I've got everything we need.

Everyone has their own papers.

At least my little beans are sleeping.

Mexico City, Mexico
Population: 8.9 million
SO BIG!
They switched to pants to try and blend in.
We need "cough" to find "cough" a shelter that has space "cough" for us. This is a big place.
Mami, you and Laura are tired. Let me search.
I'm the reason we're here. I need to do this. Is she sick or just tired?

All the shelters are full. I need to get back to them.
Think, Vilma! Is this the way?
Everything looks the same. Where are they? I'm so scared...
It'll be dark soon.
God, El Cadejo Blanco, please let me find them.

Maybe they went ahead.
She said to meet in Tijuana if we got separated.
Please, God, protect Mami and Laura and let this bus take me to them.
ENTRAL DEL SUR

There are over twenty migrant shelters in Tijuana.

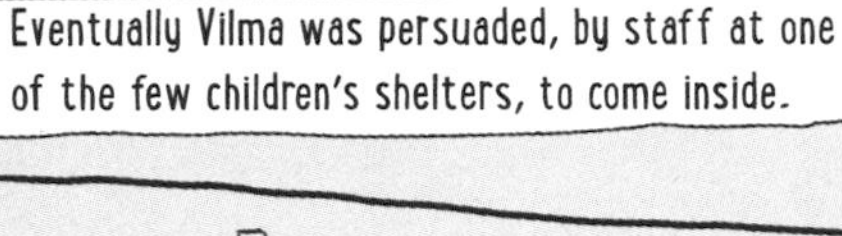

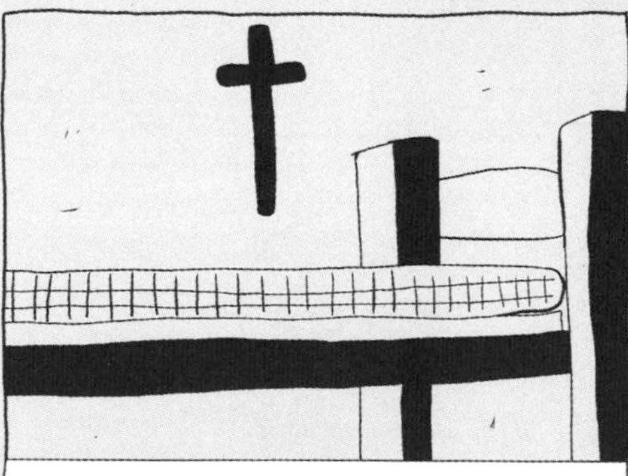

While she waited, a pro bono lawyer who worked in the US visited the shelter.

Alejandra listened carefully to Vilma's story and then helped her understand how she should cross the border and present herself to the immigration officers. Alejandra's organization would then take her case in the US.

The intakes are hard. People can get retraumatized, but the stories need to be told in detail and always retold the same way so what's written down is the same as what's said in court.

Based on Vilma's experiences, she would likely qualify for SIJS, Special Immigrant Juvenile Status. SIJS is available to minors who've been abused, neglected, or abandoned by one or both parents when reunification is not possible.

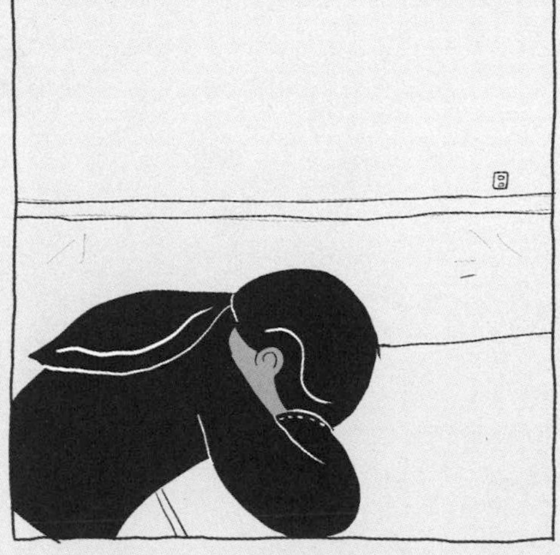

United States

Tijuana

She could be anywhere.

MEXICO

Gulf of Mexico

Mexico City

Pacific Ocean

Population of Mexico: 126 million

I don't know what to do.
I work for you, Vilma, so we can do whatever you want to do. And please remember that the legal system's slow. There's time. I'll be in Mexico and I won't stop looking for her.
Do you want to cross the border today?
Tomorrow.
Today?
Tomorrow.
Today?
Today!

CBP= Customs and Border Protection

ORR initial processing flowchart

First screening to initiate removal proceedings by government. Immigration cases are civil, not criminal, meaning there is a right to a trial, but not a lawyer.

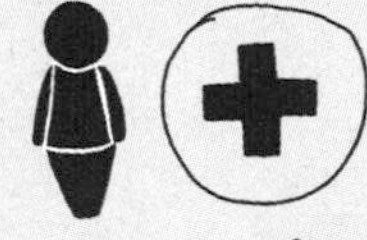

HHS provides medical checkups, immunizations, and shelter assignment.

Child transferred by DHS to HHS shelter.

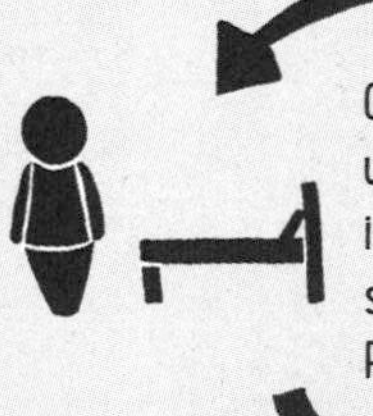

Child remains in HHS shelter until a sponsor is found. This is either a family member or someone in the Unaccompanied Refugee Minors Program.

Child is with sponsor in the US during the immigration process, which takes years.

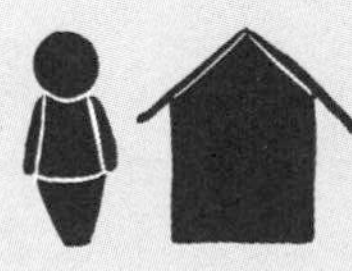

ORR= Office of Refugee Resettlement
HHS= Department of Health and Human Services
DHS= Department of Homeland Security

Vilma was transferred to a facility in Chicago. It was her first time on an airplane.

She was assigned to case workers who served as liaisons between Vilma and the lawyers.

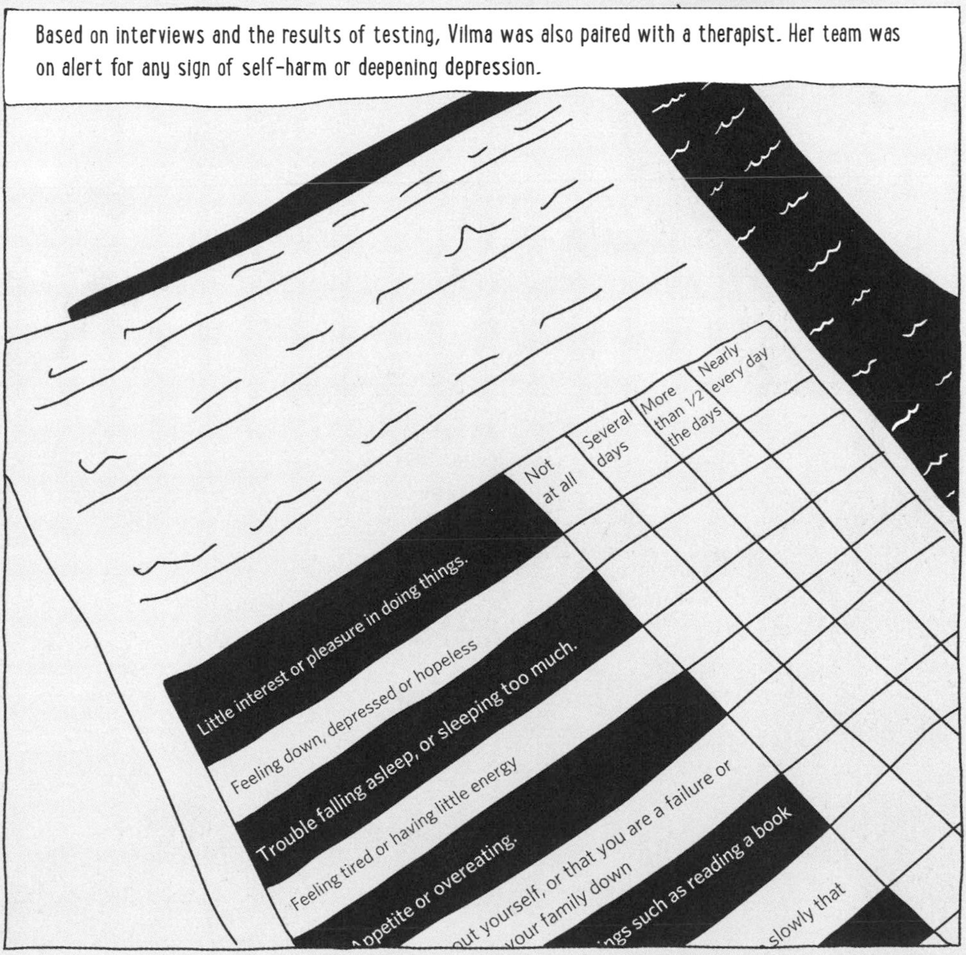

Based on interviews and the results of testing, Vilma was also paired with a therapist. Her team was on alert for any sign of self-harm or deepening depression.

Vilma was placed with a foster family within a few months. In general, a quick placement takes two to six months. All potential foster families go through a rigorous assessment and training program before any child is placed in their homes. The goal is to ensure their safety and protection.

And then it happened.

Two months after Vilma's arrival in Chicago, her mother and sister made it to Tijuana. Vilma's lawyer in Mexico, true to her word, connected them as soon as she was able.

*A temporary system of waiting for a case to be processed.

It's your fault that we're here and Mami's sick. This place smells. We're scared for our lives. There's bugs and bad people. It's all because of you that we don't have a home to go to.

She's right. It's all my fault.

If I hadn't let him...

Papa wouldn't have...

If I'd never been alive.

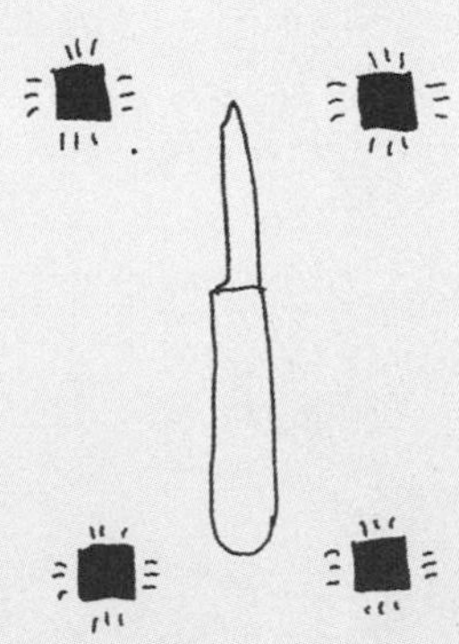

Vilma's first visit to a Spanish-speaking therapist coincided with the day she tried to cut herself.
You wanted to what? Are you saying you want to hurt yourself?
I mean I wanted to. I tried to, but I couldn't do it.
I had a knife... My soul is sick. My heart's numb.
Vilma, for your own safety I'd recommend that you go to a short-term residential hospital until you feel more stable. Would you be willing to do that?
Yeah...
This is embarrassing. What if people find out and think I'm crazy? No one talks to a doctor at home.
Vilma was admitted to a program just outside of Chicago. She was there two weeks.
There's nothing to do. So boring. And the English is very fast.
I have nobody to talk with here. Only one girl speaks Spanish and I don't like her.
It's just not my thing. I made it here on my own. I can handle myself.

After two weeks Vilma returned to her foster home.

She went back to school and started speaking weekly with her therapist.

Her mom and sister were still in Tijuana waiting for their number to come up.

And while they all waited and hoped, Vilma learned.

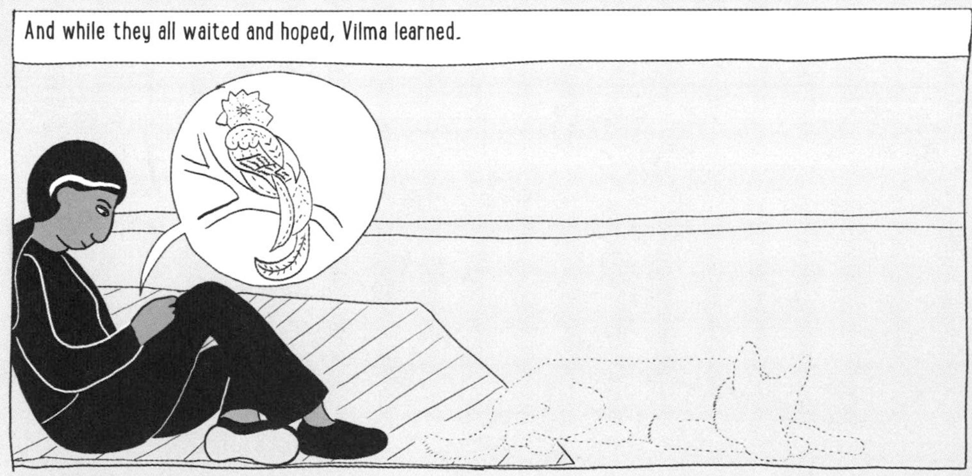

Several months later Vilma's mother and sister were allowed into the US to await their court hearings. Vilma's mom hopes to become her sponsor, so that the family can be reunited while awaiting their individual trials. According to official ORR policy the reunification of families is preferred.

Vilma continues to meet with her therapist. She still has nightmares but no longer wants to hurt herself.

She is currently in high school.

There's been no contact with her father.

Rosa

Honduras

There is always a blue sky after the storm. —Honduran proverb

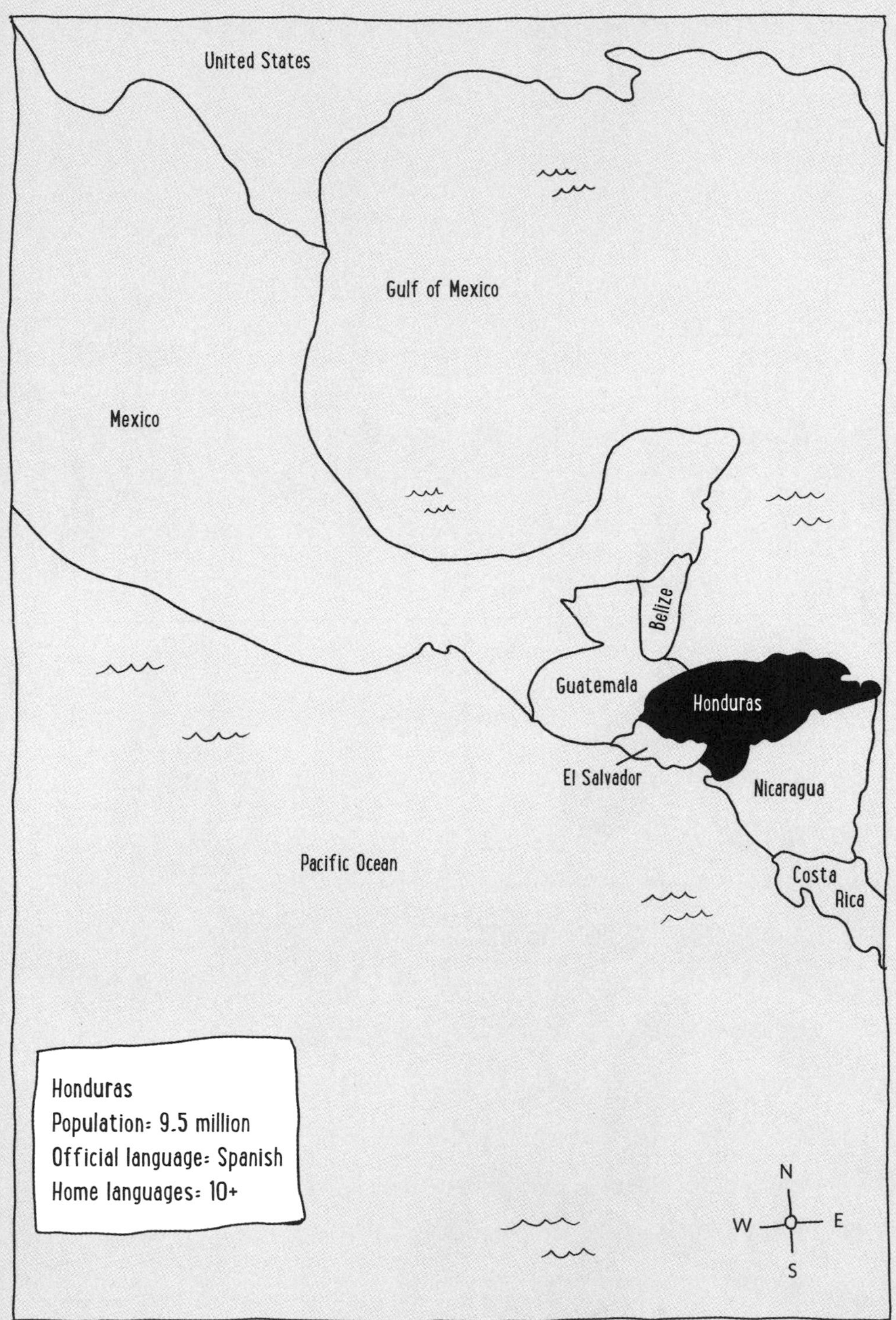
United States
Gulf of Mexico
Mexico
Belize
Guatemala
Honduras
El Salvador
Nicaragua
Pacific Ocean
Costa Rica
Honduras
Population: 9.5 million
Official language: Spanish
Home languages: 10+
N
W
E
S

Honduras, 2016

Earlier that same day

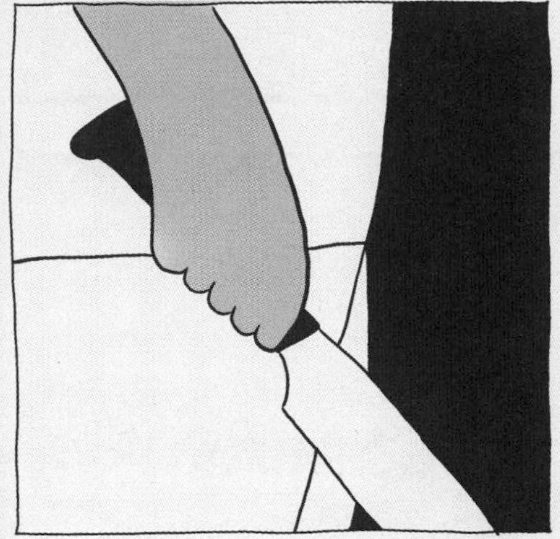

ROSA!
I swear I'm gonna cut your head off.
I sharpened my blade today. Just for you.
ROSA!

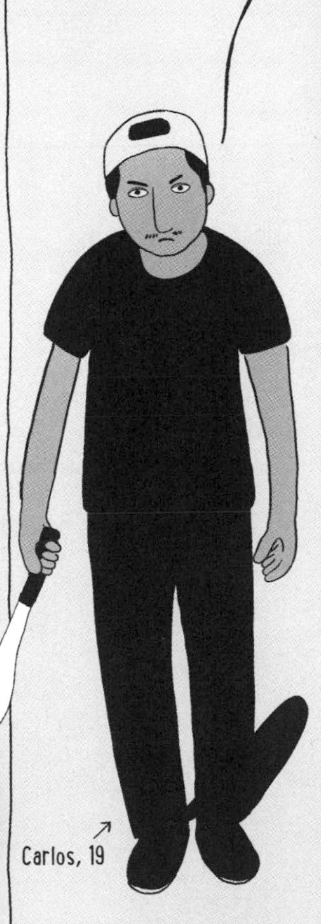

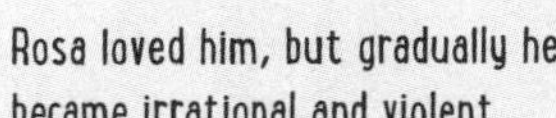

It wasn't always like this.

A few weeks earlier in Rosa's village
Is this what love feels like?
You're beautiful.
I can't believe he got this for me. And it's red, my favorite color.
No one ever bought me a new dress before.
Perfect.

Rosa left home and soon found work as a live-in housekeeper in a city several hours away.

San Pedro Sula, Honduras
Population: 719 thousand

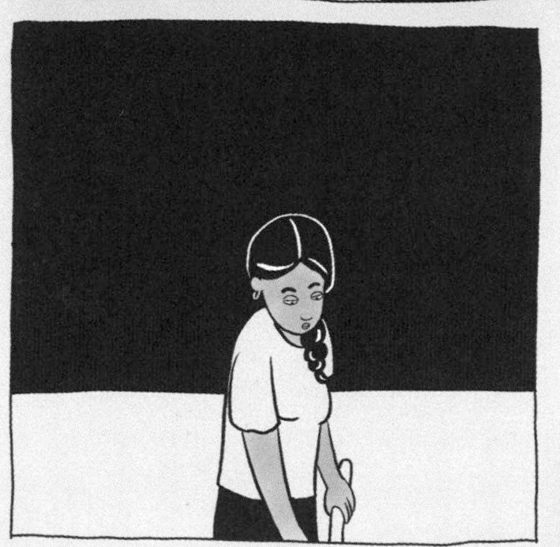

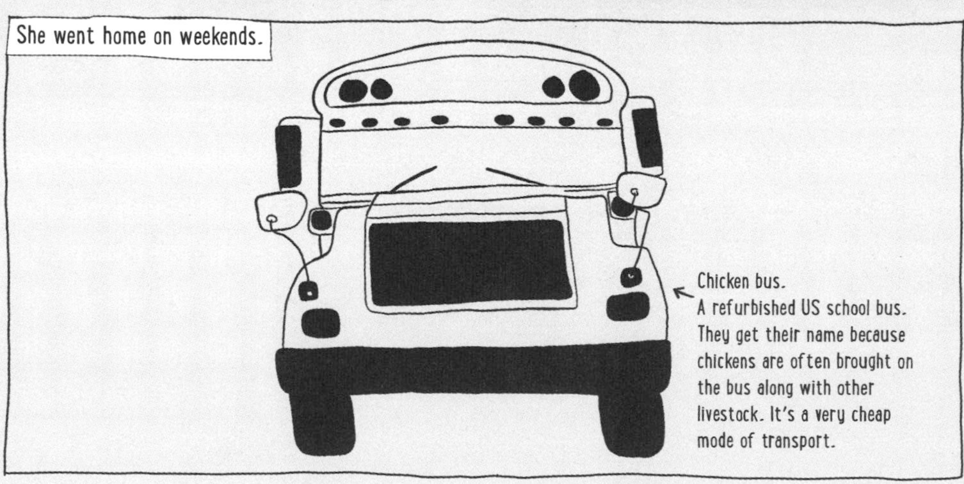
She went home on weekends.
Chicken bus.
A refurbished US school bus.
They get their name because
chickens are often brought on
the bus along with other
livestock. It's a very cheap
mode of transport.

No one ever met me when I came home.

Until.

I missed you.

But gradually things changed.

You better watch it.

He's a narco. He threatens you and forbids you to be with other people...

Rosa, it's true. Think about it.

Juana, Rosa's best friend.

No.

Drugs?!

Why's he got so much cash?

What about his temper?

He can't be...

Where does he go when he disappears?

Juana, you're right.
If I don't text him now I'll change my mind.
Sent.
We're finished.
No.
Shit.

Rosa if ur not gonna be with me, ur not gonna be with anyone.
ROSA!

Juana, it's Rosa. Let me in.

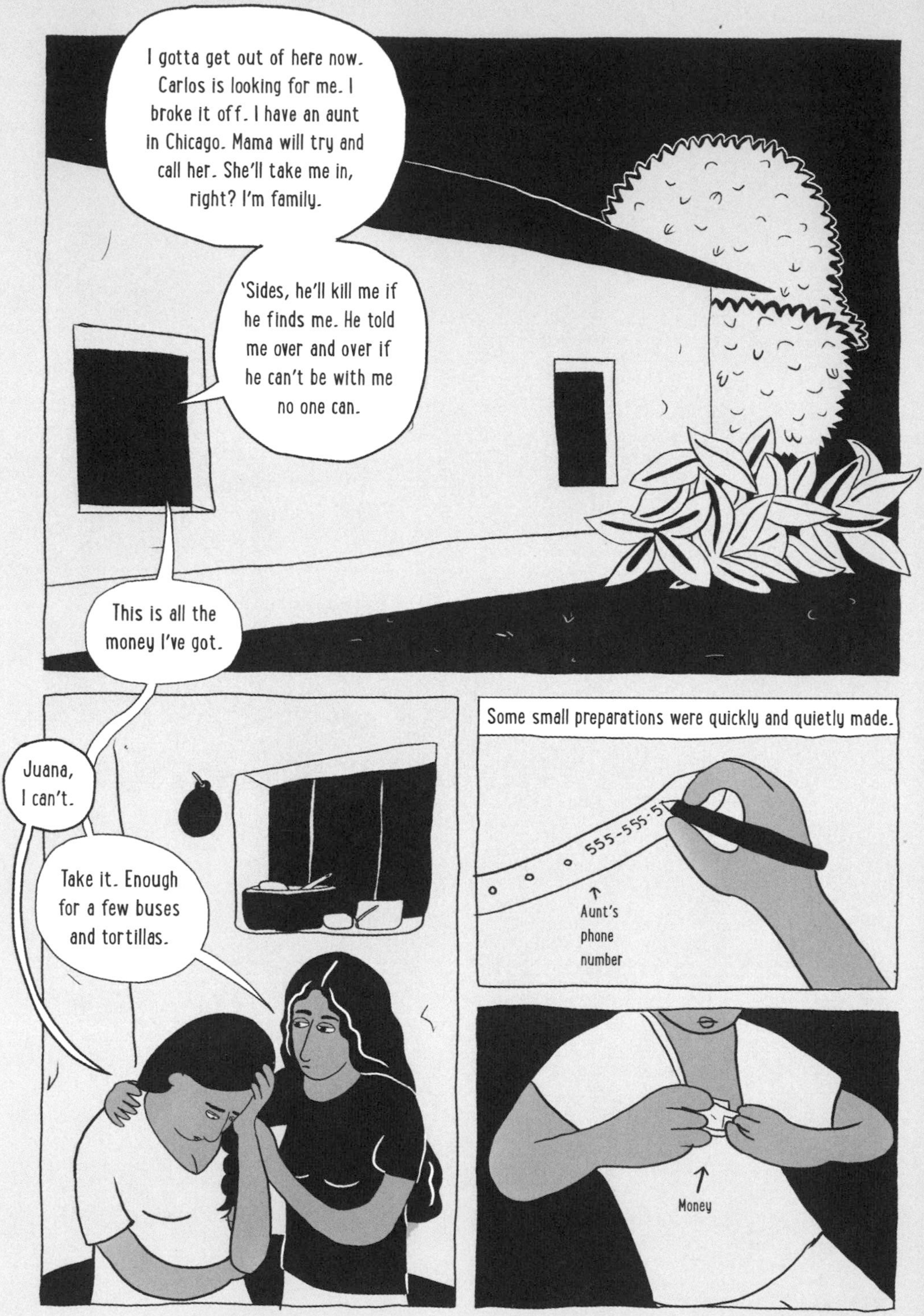

I gotta get out of here now. Carlos is looking for me. I broke it off. I have an aunt in Chicago. Mama will try and call her. She'll take me in, right? I'm family.

'Sides, he'll kill me if he finds me. He told me over and over if he can't be with me no one can.

This is all the money I've got.

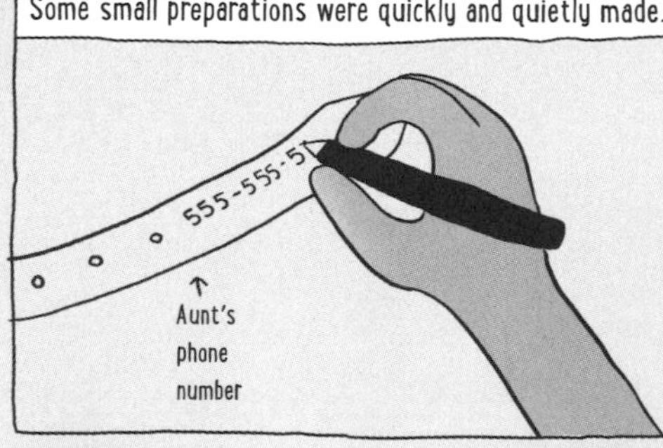

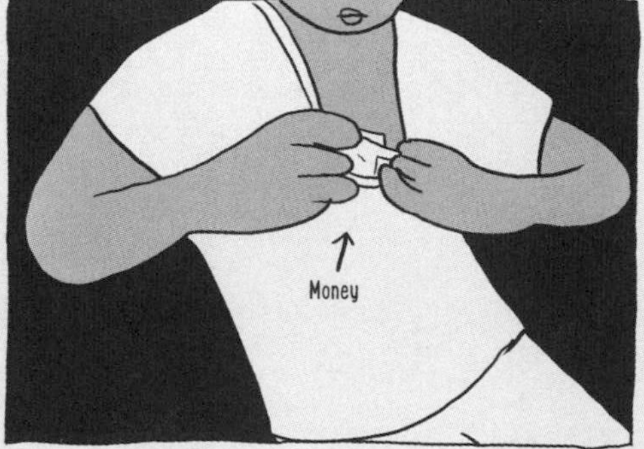

I'm strong.

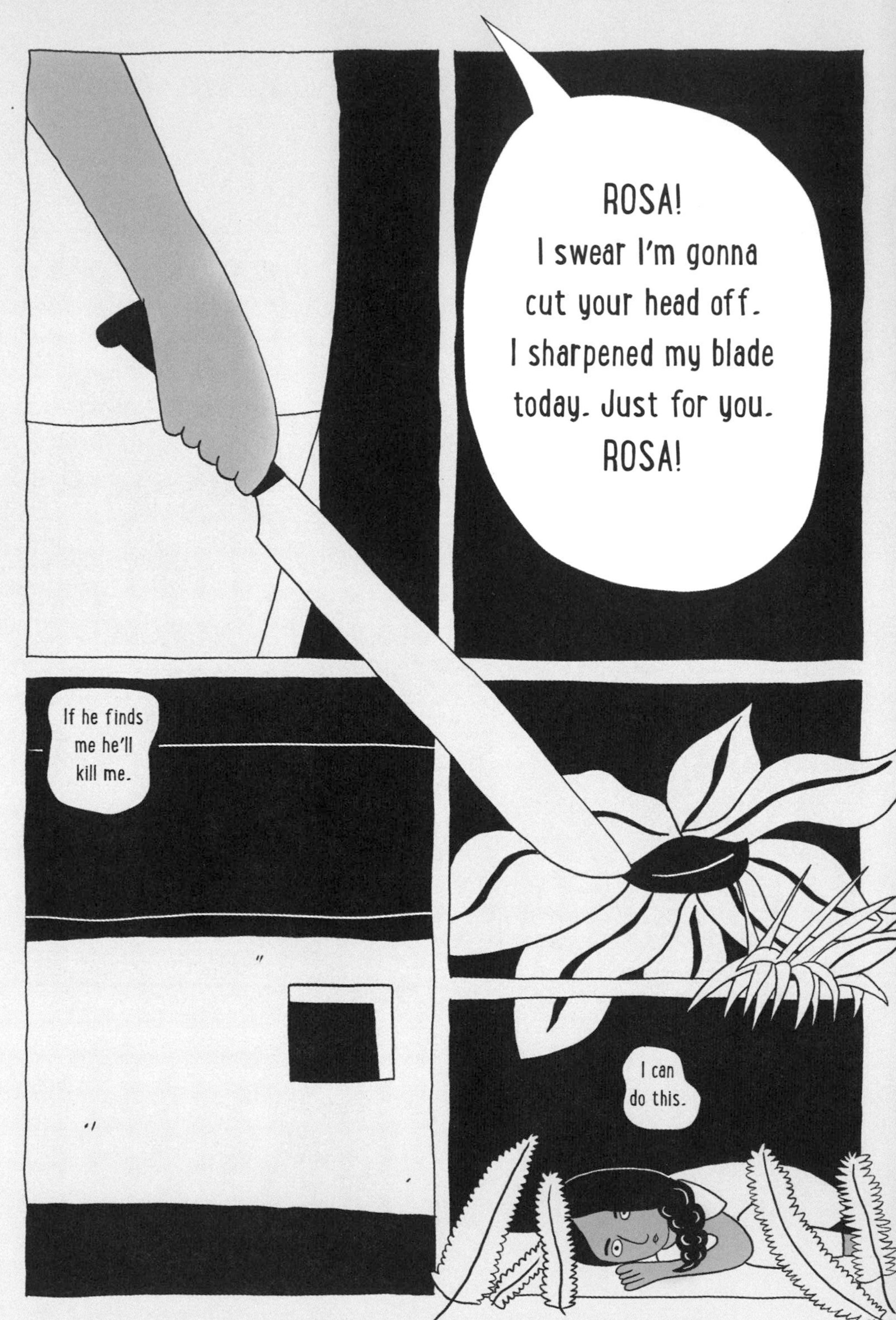
ROSA!
I swear I'm gonna cut your head off. I sharpened my blade today. Just for you. ROSA!
If he finds me he'll kill me.
I can do this.

The next morning Rosa boarded the first of several chicken buses she'd ride north on her 2,500-mile trek to the US border.

Rosa asked strangers along the way which bus to take, and where it was safe to sleep at night.
Which way is north?
Every bus
took her
closer.

Somewhere in Guatemala just south of Mexico

Almost out of money.

BIENVENIDO A MEXICO

Border patrols watch some places more than others, but there's always a way.

This rail town close to Guatemala is a starting point for riding atop cargo trains toward the US border.

Tenosique, Mexico
Population: 62 thousand

Hello.

What a sweet smile she has. Like my sisters. Kids always warm my heart.

Are you traveling alone?
Yes. Alone.
You remind me of my younger sister.
Travel with us, it's safer.
Hello!
Serious injuries or death are common when jumping on or off La Bestia.
Some riders fall off while asleep. A branch or tunnel can suddenly appear, knocking others to the ground. Gangs roam the cars. Women, girls, and trans people are often targets of violence.

Rosa and the family traveled together for days. Their schedule was dictated by La Bestia. Whether in the middle of the night or the heat of the day, when it growled they were ready.
Each time a train line ended they waited for a new train. Eating when they could. Free food from migrant shelters and kind people at the track edges.
I'll find food.
Bless you, Rosa. I don't think another train's coming for a while.

Getting on a
A man Rosa traveled with.

Please, God, watch over him.

moving train

Please

isn't easy.

make it.

Every day people
Almost!
are injured.
He's got the handle. Wait...!
or die...
NOOOOO
NOOOOOOOOOOOOOOOOOOO
Don't look back. Don't look back. Don't look back.

Rosa got off the next time the train stopped.

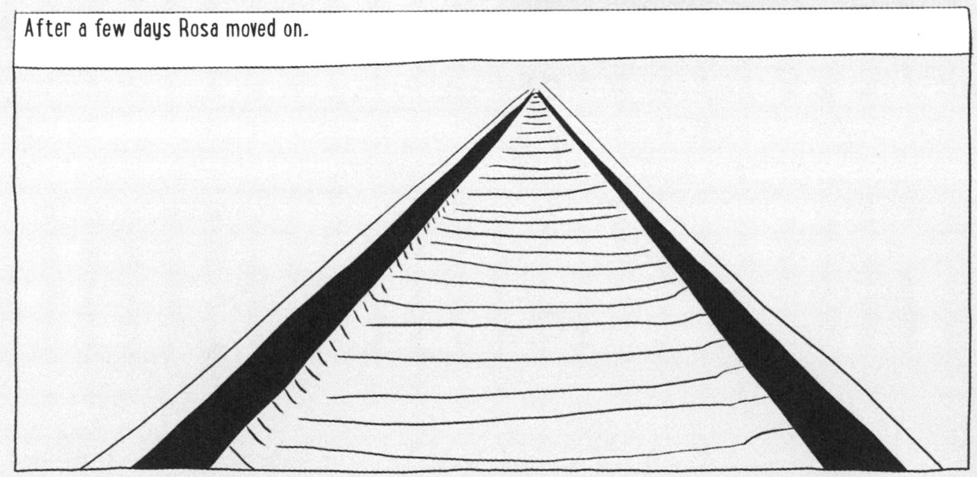

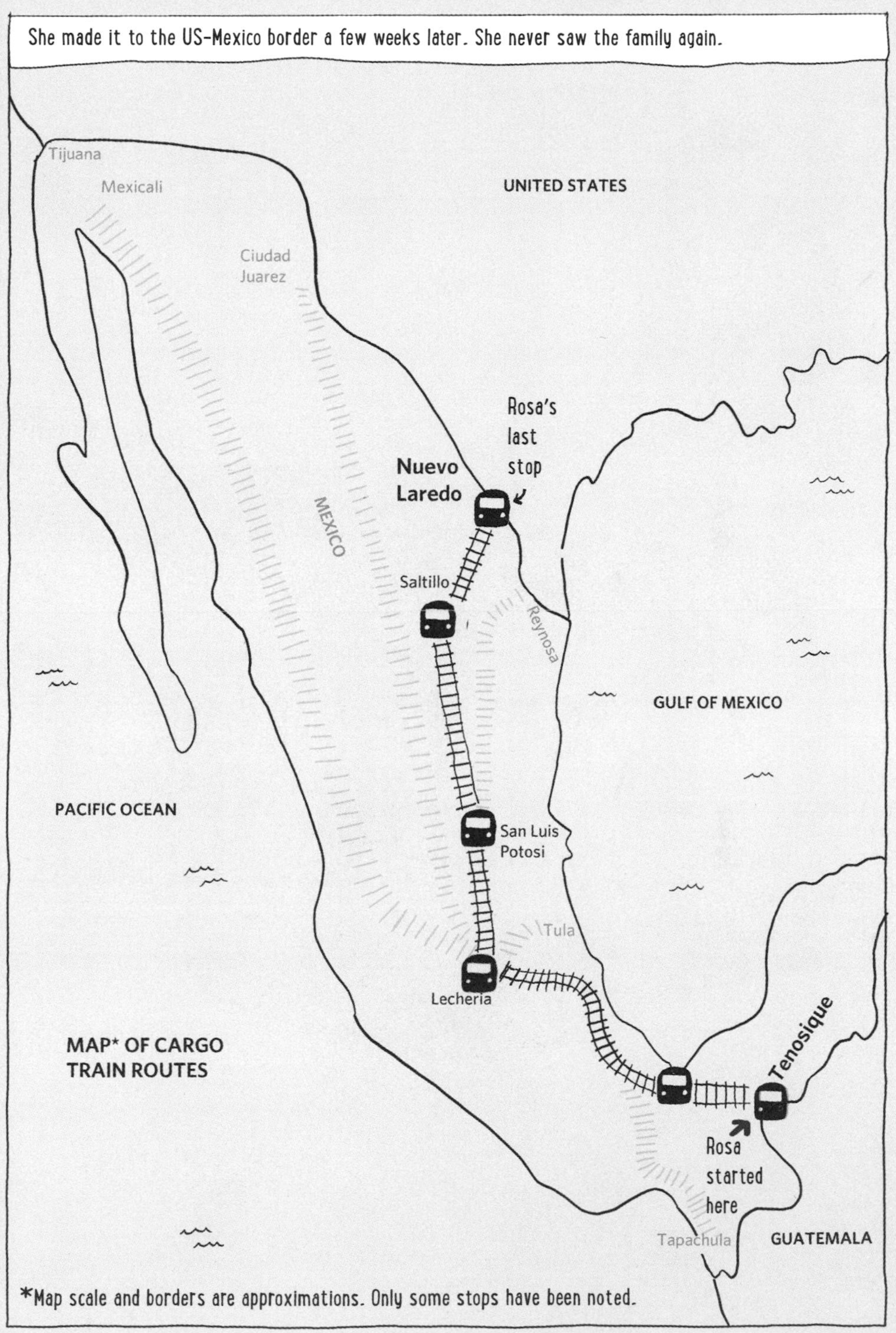
She made it to the US-Mexico border a few weeks later. She never saw the family again.
Tijuana
Mexicali
UNITED STATES
Ciudad Juarez
MEXICO
Rosa's last stop
Nuevo Laredo
Saltillo
Reynosa
GULF OF MEXICO
PACIFIC OCEAN
San Luis Potosi
Tula
Lecheria
MAP* OF CARGO TRAIN ROUTES
Tenosique
Rosa started here
Tapachula
GUATEMALA
*Map scale and borders are approximations. Only some stops have been noted.

She asked fellow travelers where to cross. La Migra* picked her up within a few hours.

*Immigration

For Rosa, and any URM (unaccompanied refugee minor) seeking legal refuge in the United States, getting picked up by La Migra quickly means not dying in the desert or becoming prey to gangs. It does mean being placed into the US immigration system.

How someone becomes a sponsor for an unaccompanied child*:

ORR (Office of Refugee Resettlement) officials locate the parent or relative.

Potential sponsor undergoes background check and completes sponsor assessment. This process identifies risk factors and other potential safety concerns.

Potential sponsor undergoes criminal public record check and, in most cases, a sex offender registry check. In some instances a home study is also required.

If there is a safety concern for release to a related sponsor or when considering release to an unrelated sponsor, ORR also conducts background checks on adult household members and individuals identified in a potential sponsor's care plan.

If potential sponsor is in compliance with Congress's directive to ensure the safety and suitability of potential sponsor, child is released to the sponsor.

*According to the Office of Refugee Resettlement

Rosa's aunt didn't know Rosa was on her way until she got the call from the ORR.

Chicago

As soon as Rosa was registered as an unaccompanied minor at the border, deportation proceedings began.

Rosa, you've got the right to a trial, but not a lawyer, so we provide free council.
We go to immigration court and find kids who need representation. We also work directly with the shelters. That's how we connected with Rosa.
Claudia, a bilingual lawyer from one of the few nonprofits that advocates for URM, was assigned to Rosa's case.

To make the legal case for asylum, Rosa had to tell her story repeatedly to Claudia.

He was violent...
And would be required to tell it in court, no matter how retraumatizing.

She also had to think about her education.
chool attendance is ndatory and supports our case by showing u're responsible and e positive intentions.

School? But I don't even speak English yet.

Rosa was placed in ESL classes with students from around the world. As part of school protocol, she reported to the nurse her first few weeks there.

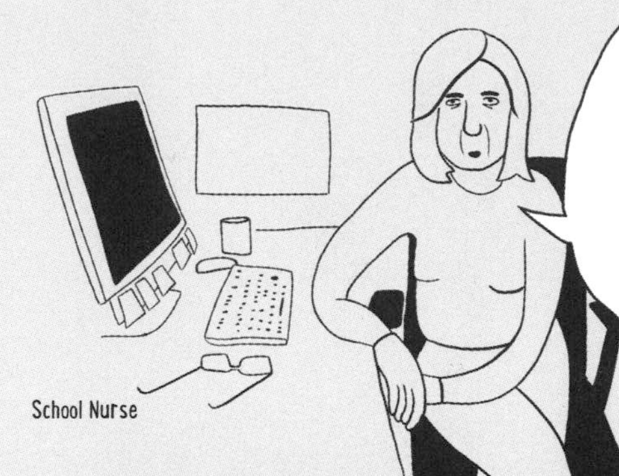

One week later

*The third largest minority population in Honduras, the Garufina, are often targets of racism.

*ORR pays for medical costs while children are in the system.

A few weeks later Aunt Sylvia got the mail early.

I took you in. No idea you were coming. Spend money on you, and you bring a filthy disease in here to get me sick too?!

I'm sorry, this isn't what...
Isn't what?

I didn't mean, I didn't know.

What?
You're not going to contaminate my house. You hear me.
You brought this on yourself.
OUT!! I WANT YOU OUT NOW!

I want YOU gone. Never come back. NEVER speak to me again. You bring shame to this family.

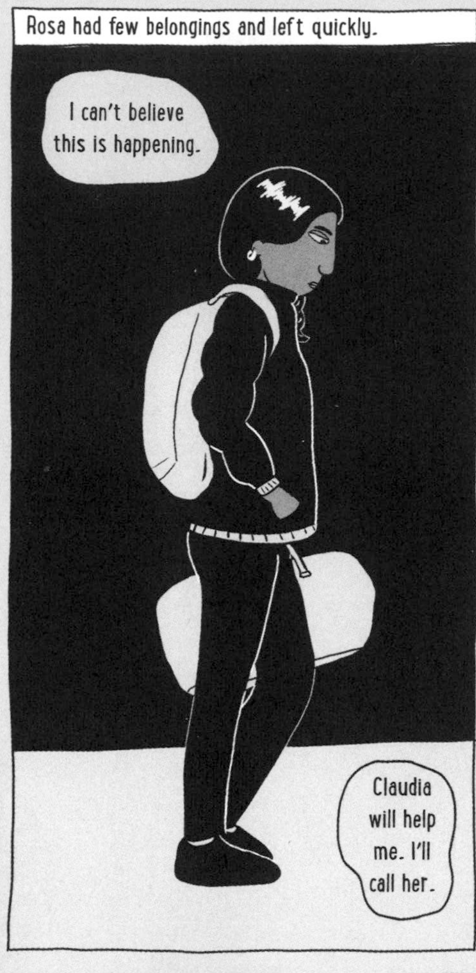
Rosa had few belongings and left quickly.
I can't believe this is happening.
Claudia will help me. I'll call her.

Which way should I go?

...teen shelter... I'll meet you at... take the... We'll get through this, Rosa.

I didn't think it'd be so big.

I can do this.

I'm ready to go in.

Rosa was granted asylum on the basis of her HIV status and her credible fear of Carlos.

Her dream of becoming a mom came true. She and her partner and their daughter live outside Chicago. Rosa is focused on her health and young family. She wants to complete her education when her daughter is old enough to go to school.

Rosa remains estranged from her aunt but occasionally talks to her mom on the phone. Her mom does not know she is HIV positive.

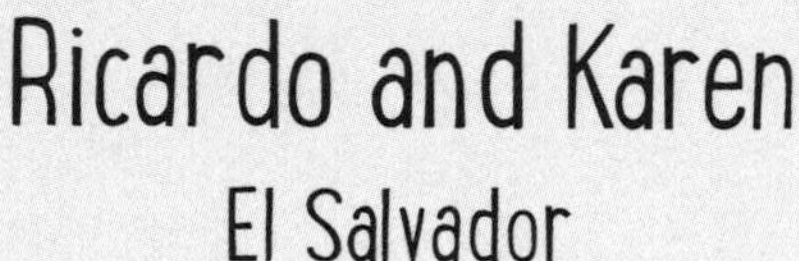

Once more there'll be peace/ but of a different kind. —Claribel Alegria, "The Return"

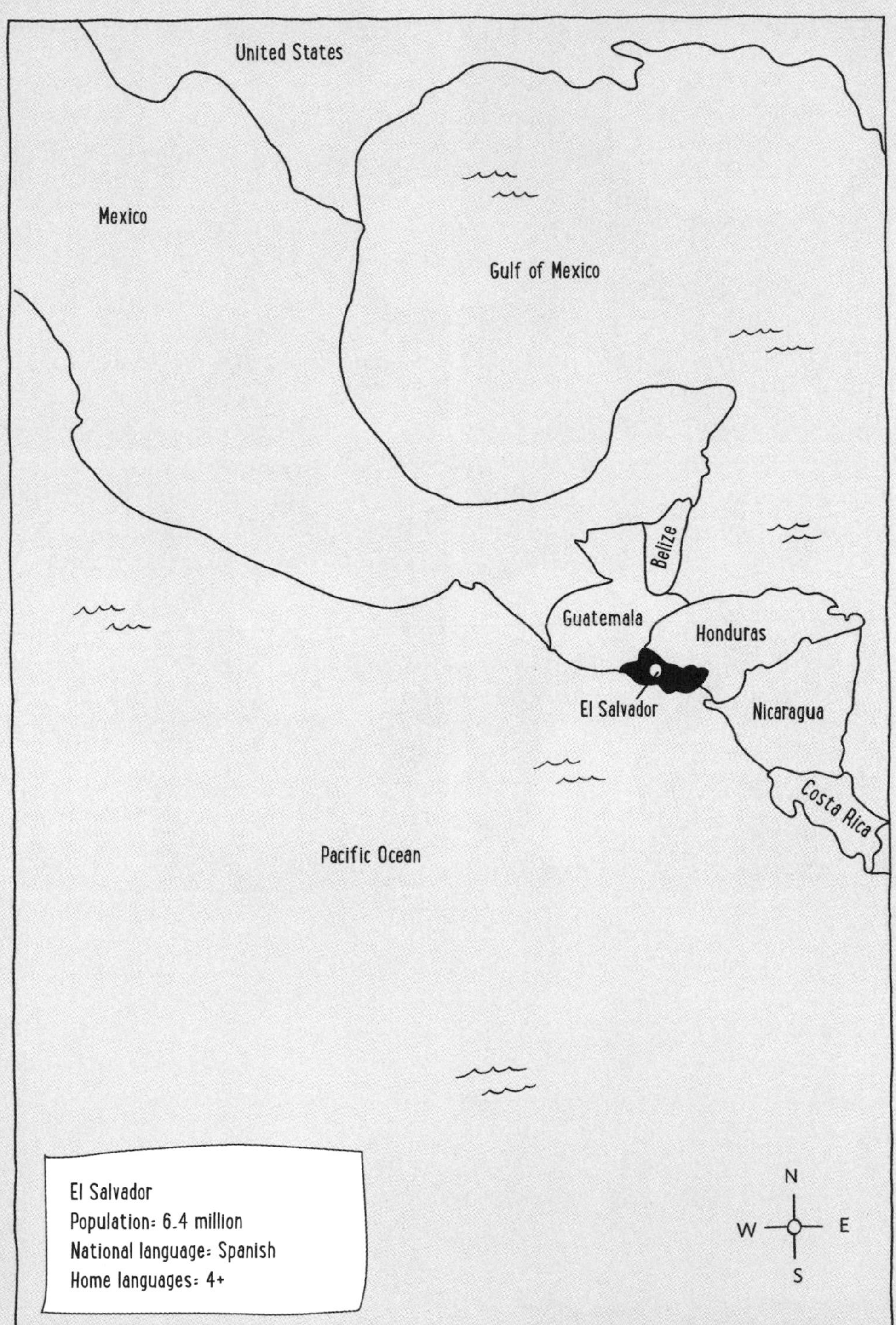
United States
Mexico
Gulf of Mexico
Belize
Guatemala
Honduras
El Salvador
Nicaragua
Costa Rica
Pacific Ocean
El Salvador
Population: 6.4 million
National language: Spanish
Home languages: 4+
N
W
E
S

A small town in El Salvador, 2014

Everything was peaceful in their neighborhood until things started to happen in 2011.

Ricardo and Karen's maternal family had lived in the village for generations. Their dad died when they were small. Their mom worked on a coffee plantation an hour's walk away, leaving Cardo to care for his sister.

First it was two strangers who recruited the most desperate children, then threats and demands for protection money started. More strangers appeared. It was like an invasion that couldn't be stopped.

In their town, local gangs are under the control of MS1 (La Mara Salvatrucha), a multinational organization that originated in Los Angeles in the 1980s and spread down through Central America.

What, you don't like me?! If you don't join we'll kill you. Die or live, your choice.

It's time.

But we pay you Renta* every month, on time! I promise we won't say anything. Please just leave us alone.

I won't become like you.

*La Renta is a protection tax imposed by the gangs.

Standing their ground and saying no culminated in a final threat.

They're gonna kill us for sure.

They won't leave us alone till they get what they want.

We were stupid to think they'd leave us alone.

What're we gonna do?

Mama'll be home soon, Karen.

We have to leave tonight I think.

Once Mama came home, decisions were made.

We can't stay here. They'll be coming for us.
But where can we go?
El Norte.
Mama, what about you?
El Norte. Yes, they won't reach you there.
I'll stay so they think you're here. You two'll go ahead. They don't want me.

I have Uriel's number. He's an old friend. He'll take care of you when you get there.
I'll call Esteban. He's been North, he knows what to do.
He says take buses. They're safest. No trains, whatever you do don't take La Bestia.

Tonight you''ll leave.

Take as little as possible so you blend in.
Toothbrush. Toothpaste. Sweater. Birth certificates.
God will protect and bless you both.
I know the two of you can make it. Ricardo will take care of you, Karen.
Mami, come with us please.
We'll meet in the US and finally be safe.

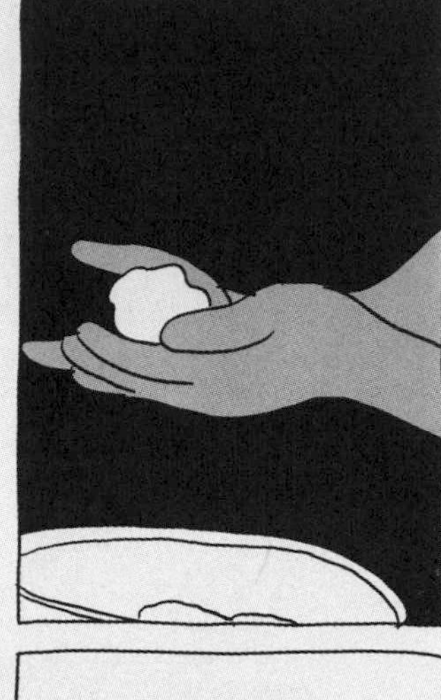

Pupusa, national dish of El Salvador.

Made with corn flour and cheese plus beans, meat, or vegetables.

God protect my children and take care of them on their journey.

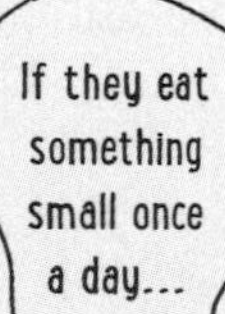

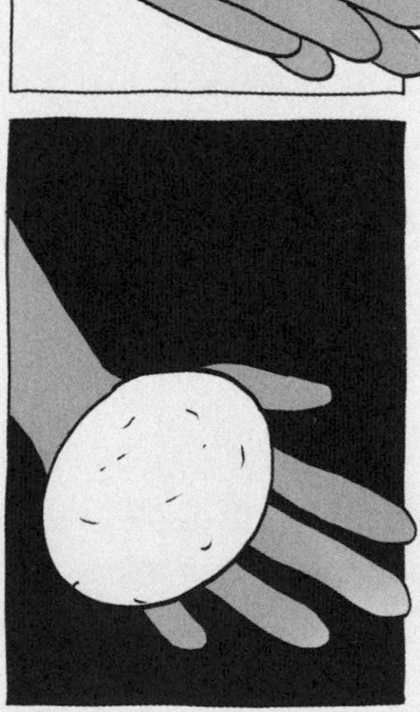

Best eaten warm.

Each of you carry a little money so it's not all in one place.
Depend on me, Mama. I'll protect us both.
Karencita, we'll walk quietly and quickly. Talk to no one. Heads down.
Memorize Uriel's number.
Leave before dawn.

What if I can't protect her...
Every step we take is another step away from everything we know.
Have a pupusa while it's still warm. Your favorite with loroco.
The last one we'll be able to eat here.

They traveled north.

With the money their mother gave them, they headed toward Mexico.
41

They slept when and where they could.
23

And then their cash ran out.
Karen, wake up. We have to get moving.
Morning already?

They stayed for several weeks, working and sleeping on the street until they had enough money to continue by bus to Tijuana.

After several more bus rides, they arrived in Tijuana.

Mama said not to talk to anyone, but he's around the same age as me, maybe younger. He's looking me in the eye. That's a good sign.
Want some food?
Come on, I invite you.
He's friendly. If he were bad, he wouldn't be so nice.
What do we do? Karen needs food. I need food. We have to do something.
So are you staying here or moving on?

I'll help you...
for a fee.

How much?

How much
ya got?

Umm... this much.
That'll do for now. Once you cross you can work and send the rest. What do you say?
My sister and I need to talk.

I know people who can get you through this last part. I'll cross you and guarantee the trip.
I have a sister too, I know what it's like.
We trust you, we just need to talk.
Can we trust him?
Trust me.
Mami said not to talk to anyone.
Can we trust him?

Coyotes are human smugglers. They're paid to guide people safely through Mexico from other countries and/or get them illegally across the border.

Everyone wants the American dream. If you don't make it across on the first try, I'll even help you one more time, no extra money.

Coyotes are an expensive and dangerous gamble. They can charge upward of $2,000 USD and generally work for gangs. Often they take money and disappear, or hold people for ransom or hurt them.

Sometimes they bring people (including children) to remote locations and abandon them in the desert without resources.

Dehydration can be deadly. There are organizations that leave water jugs in the desert on known paths to the US, and others that find and identify human remains, which can then be returned to the families searching for their missing relatives.

After a short discussion, Ricardo and Karen came to an agreement.

He took them down several streets to the meeting place. Smugglers typically cram as many people as possible into a vehicle to maximize profits.

And then, somewhere near the base of Otay Mountain, a 3,566-foot peak crawling with rattlesnakes, the van stopped.
Everyone out! Run, go, go, get out...
Fortunately they were dropped near a known patrol spot and quickly processed.
Do you have relatives in the US?
Yes.

As it turned out, the "uncle," or distant family friend, did not remember the connection or didn't want to remember it.

Ricardo and Karen remained in San Diego.

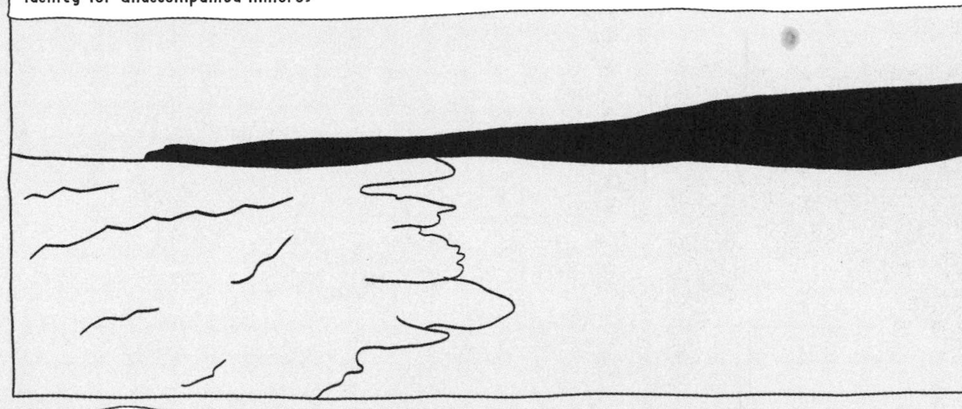

Shelters by law (Flores Settlement, 1997) must support children with medical and mental health care, recreational activities, and educational offerings like basic English. Unaccompanied Refugee Minors aren't allowed to enroll directly in public school while living in shelters and can only leave the grounds with shelter officials to attend court proceedings or visits with legal counsel.

Within a few weeks there were regular meetings with pro bono lawyers from a local San Diego nonprofit to prepare Karen and Ricardo's cases. They were hopeful.

Until it wasn't.

Under federal guidelines, Ricardo aged out of the minor system when he turned eighteen. His lawyers tried to keep him where he was, but couldn't.

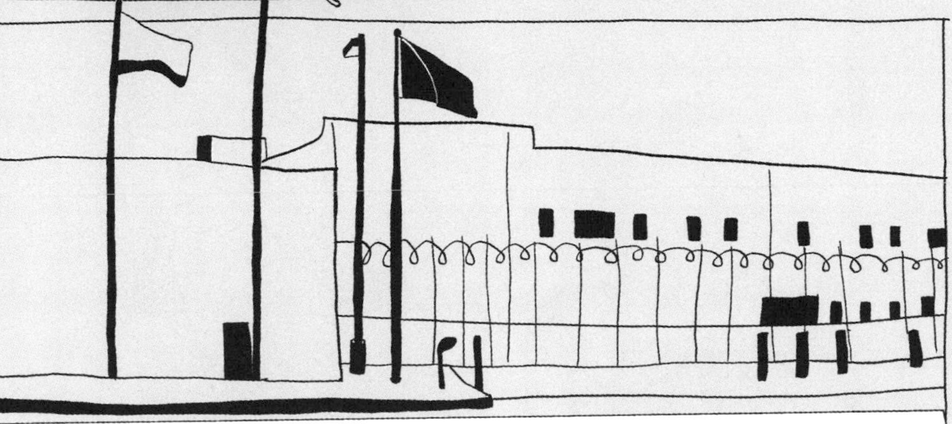

And just like that, Ricardo was placed with adults.

A few weeks later.

Suddenly there was new hope. Karen's mother, at the advice of her lawyer, submitted an asylum case too.

But a judge felt differently. 71% of all adult asylum cases are denied.

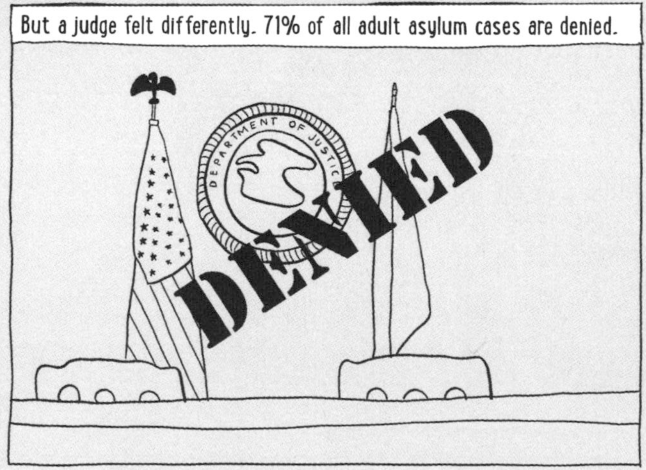

Ricardo's case fared no better.

Karen, listen. I've spoken with Cardo. We want you to stay.
I want you to be safe.
No, Mami, please...
You have the chance for a life here, for a future.
At home, there's nothing but danger.

Karen was placed with a long-term sponsor family in the Midwest. She's attending school there and waiting as her case slowly winds its way through the courts. The average length of asylum cases in immigration court is over three years.

Ricardo and his mother were deported. The original lawyer for Ricardo lost track of him and no longer has contact with Karen.

Currently there's no specific tracking data on what happens to people fleeing gang violence who are sent back to their home country.

Fanta

Guinea

No matter how long the winter, spring is sure to follow. —Guinean proverb

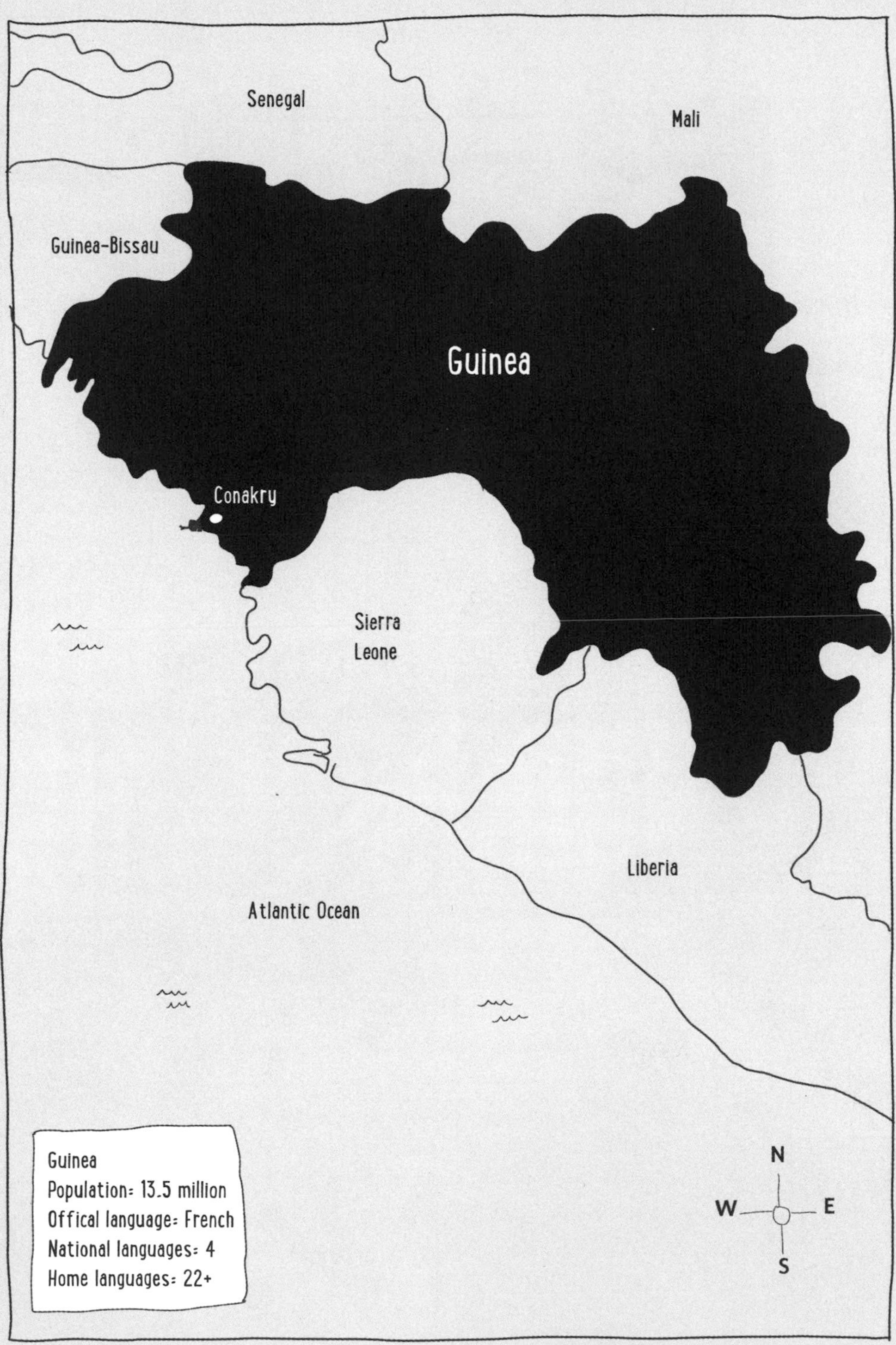
Senegal
Mali
Guinea-Bissau
Guinea
Conakry
Sierra
Leone
Liberia
Atlantic Ocean
Guinea
Population: 13.5 million
Offical language: French
National languages: 4
Home languages: 22+
N
W
E
S

Guinea, 2015

Conakry
Population: 2 million
Papa, I wish you could see your grandson. He looks like you and my brothers.
Fanta, 13
Oumar, 2 days old
May Allah instill blessings on you, Oumar.
I'll keep you safe always.

2014, a rural village several hours from Conakry

Fanta's father died from an infection when she was nine. Her uncle, as is the custom in her village, became head of the household and made all family decisions.

The nikah, the signing of the marriage contract, was done at a mosque in Conakry. Fanta's presence was not required and she wasn't there.

Fanta would now live with her husband, away from her mother, brothers, and community.

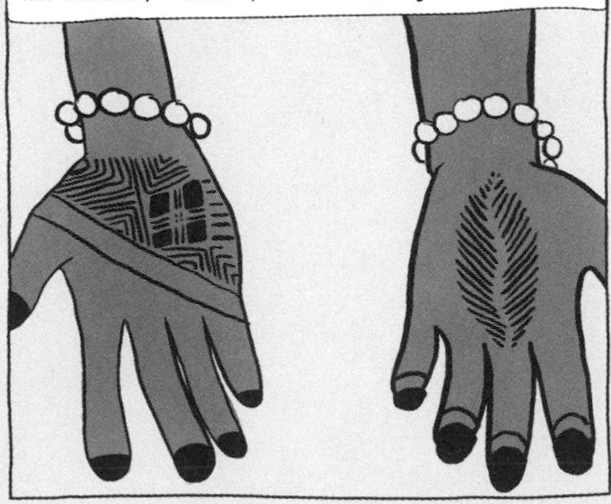

The walima, the marriage banquet, happened a few weeks later at her husband's home in Conakry.

And then, it was time...

Why doesn't he smile?

Your husband awaits you!

May your children be Muslim!

He was forty. Fanta was twelve.

He looks older than Uncle.

Please be nice, please be nice.

Please... I don't want to.
You're my wife now and you'll do as I say.
NO PLEASE...
YES!

She's a beautiful bride.

Praise Allah!

At least my mother won't witness my misery.

It wasn't just the physical abuse and rape on Fanta's wedding night that caused so much agony.

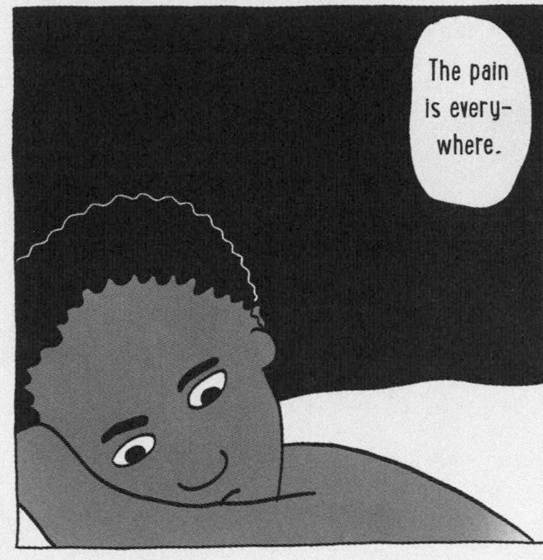

I was so young when they cut me, I don't remember it.

For some communities in Guinea, cutting is a cultural and traditional ceremony that is a rite of passage for girls.

97% of all women and girls between 15 and 49 have been through genital cutting in Guinea.

Sexual intercourse is often painful for those who have undergone the rite.

The government has enacted legislation to prevent female genital mutilation (FGM). However, it is still endorsed by some religious and political leaders. FGM is any procedure that involves partial or total removal of the external female genitalia or other injury to the female genital organs for nonmedical reasons.*

*As defined by the World Health Organization.

Aminata, Fanta's trusted older friend from her village, lived in Conakry as well. It made her move more bearable. Aminata married for love. Her husband was kind and supportive.

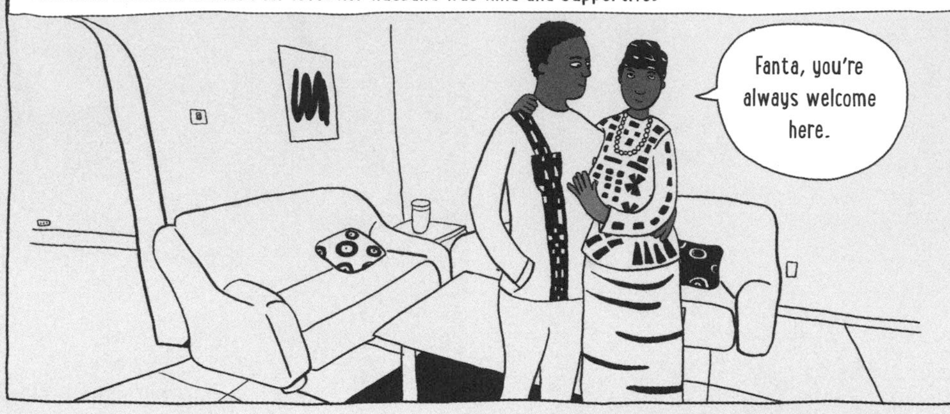

Luckily, her village community gave Fanta a way. Following tradition, Fanta returned to her childhood home to recuperate after giving birth.

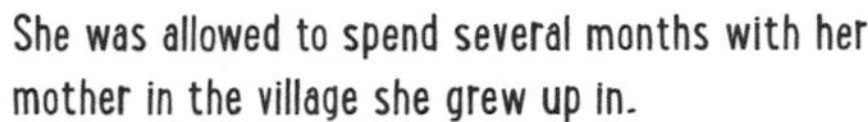

Nothing changed.

FANTA!!!!

Every day Fanta

hoped that things would

get better.
HAS YOUR MOTHER TAUGHT YOU NOTHING!!!

But they only
No school. Your place is in my house.

got worse.
This millet is runny!

Every evening was the same.
Come to our room NOW!
At first I fought him.
He ripped off my clothes and beat me.
Then I realized that's what he wanted.
My refusal to make a sound only angered him more.
But Allah is with me always so I can stay strong. He won't break me.

The beatings were so terrible Fanta sought outside help. Something unheard of in her community.
REPUBLIQUE DE GUINEA
COMMISSARIAT CENTRAL DE POLICE DE MATOTO
POLICE

My husband hits me every day.
Please help me.

Go home. This is a family matter not for the police.

So Fanta went back.

And then the unthinkable happened.
Can you see what Oumar needs?
MAAAAAAMMMMMAAAAAAA
I see what he needs.
Now I know it's not just me he doesn't love.

One year later, another miracle.
The abuse only stopped after her daughter Mariame was born.
Mariame
And that was because Fanta returned to be with her mother in the village where she grew up.
Mama, Allah will show me the path to take, but I know it's not back to him.
My children can't grow up around that.

So Fanta, defying hundreds of years of tradition, did not return to her husband.

Bless you both for letting us stay at your house.

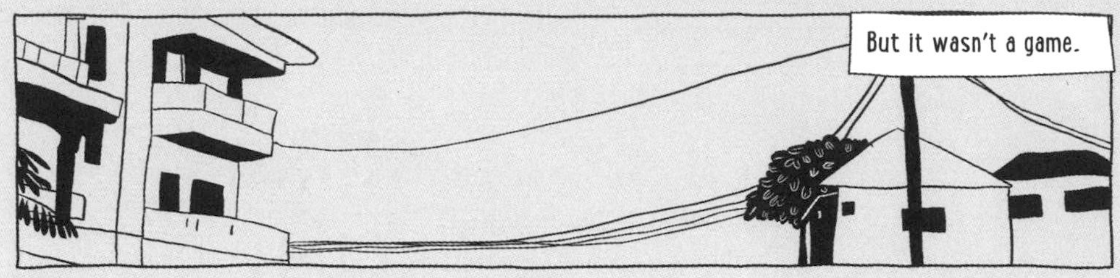

After several months, Fanta's husband realized she was not returning. He had no interest in the children as he had others from his first wife, and they were more mouths to feed. But the longer she stayed away, the more foolish he looked. Soon his relatives were calling Fanta with insults.

You're bringing shame to your family.

Enough!

Go back!

Didn't your mother teach you to be a good Muslim?

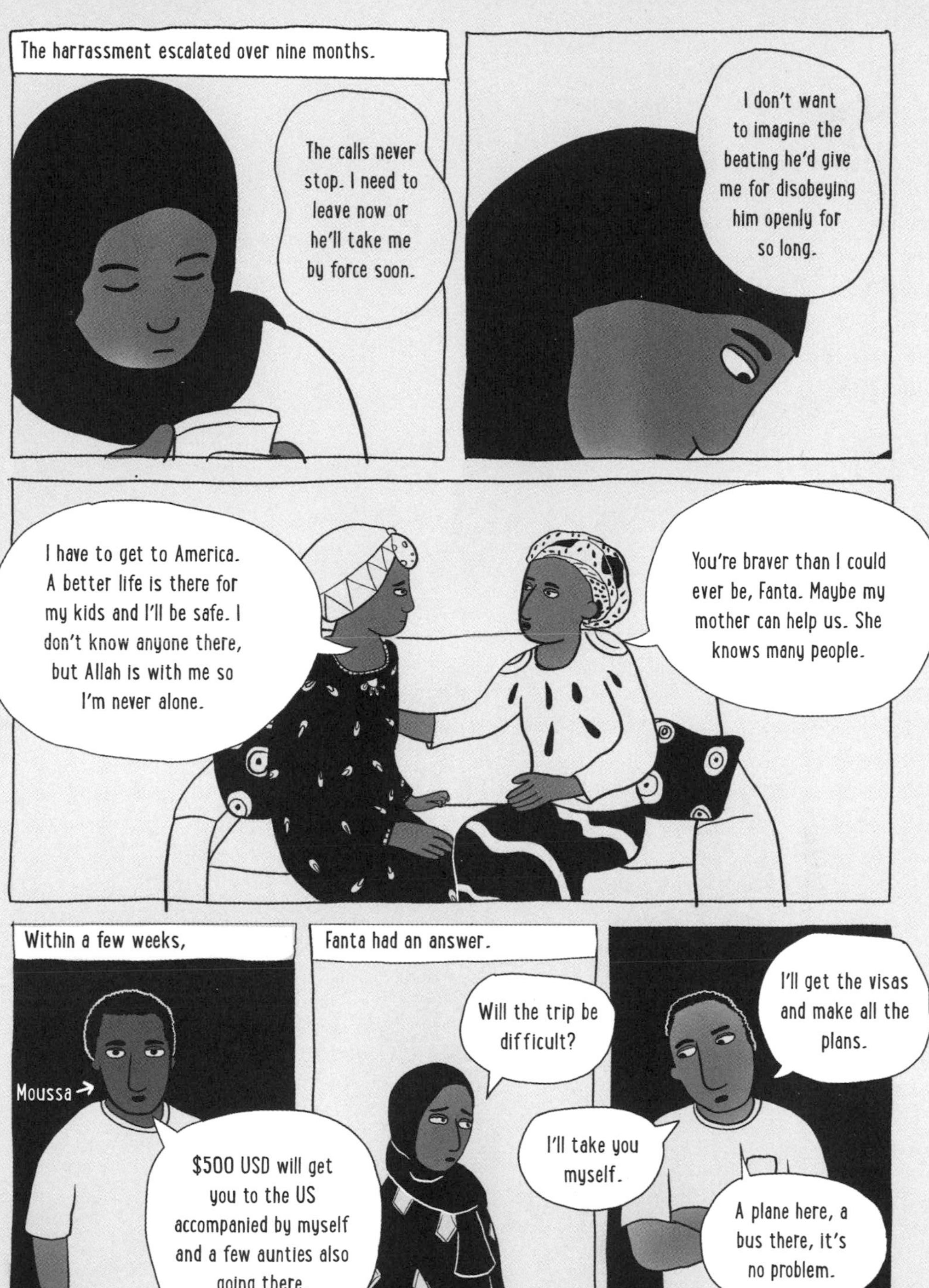

*The average salary per year in Guinea is $10,000 USD.

It took Fanta almost two years to save enough money. She was sixteen. The hardest thing she did by far was to leave her children with her mother. Her only solace was knowing that her husband's disinterest in them, and the cost of keeping them, would prevent him from taking them back.

She met Moussa at the airport. It was Fanta's first time leaving Guinea, her first time on a plane, and her first time without family or friends.

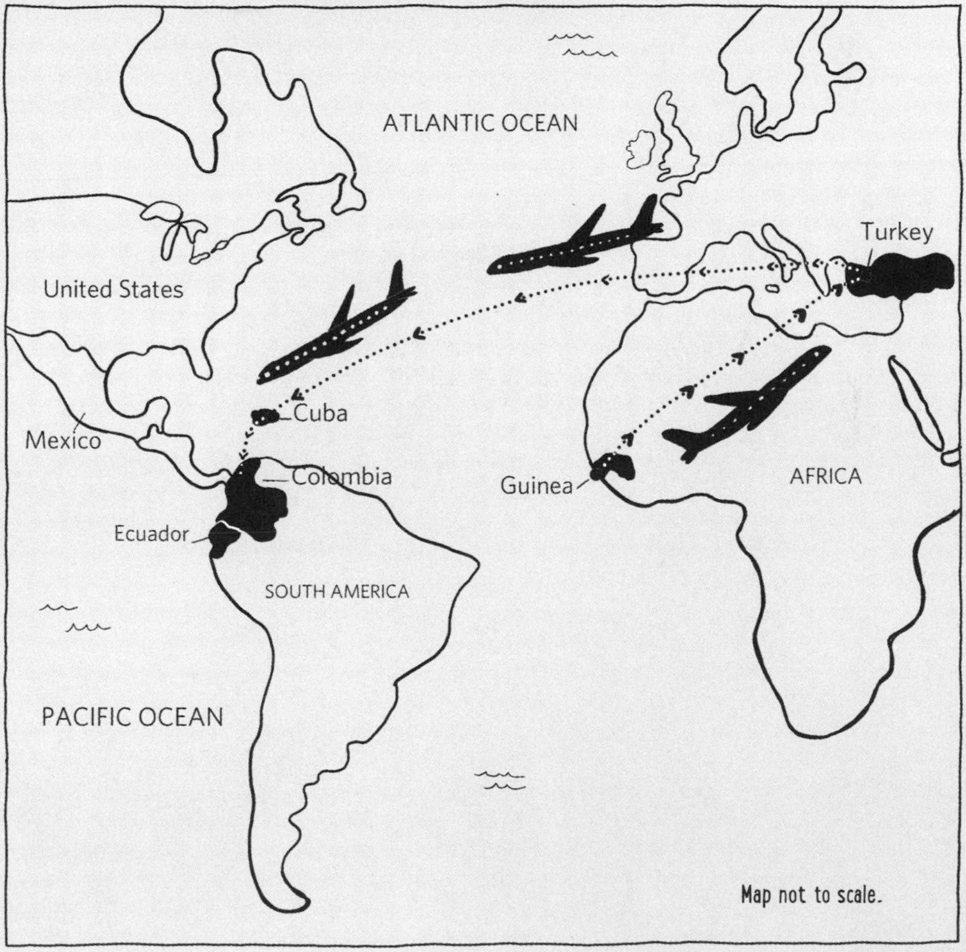

ATLANTIC OCEAN

Turkey

United States

Cuba

Mexico

Colombia

Guinea

AFRICA

Ecuador

SOUTH AMERICA

PACIFIC OCEAN

Map not to scale.

After flights to Turkey and to Cuba,
she finally ended up in Colombia.

El Dorado International Airport, Bogotá

As a devout Muslim, Fanta prayed five times a day, but during the journey she prayed when she could.

Why do you do that here? you'll bring eyes upon us!

A local guide met them in Colombia and disappeared after they paid him. Moussa, who'd done the trip before, decided to take them through anyway.

There was enough food for one meal a day. If all went well it would take them five days.

Everywhere they went, danger lurked.

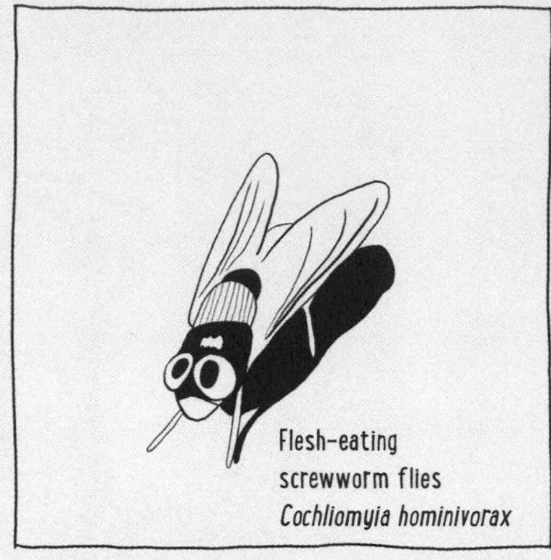

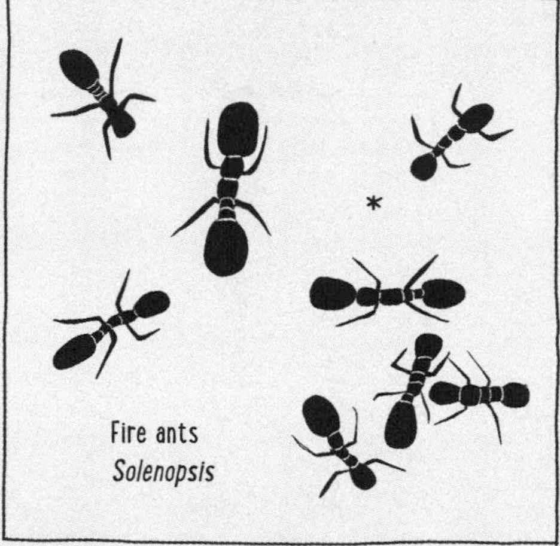

They walked from 6:00 AM to 7:00 PM in oppressive heat, only stopping for short water breaks. On the second day they began the treacherous ascent up Montaña de la Muerte*.

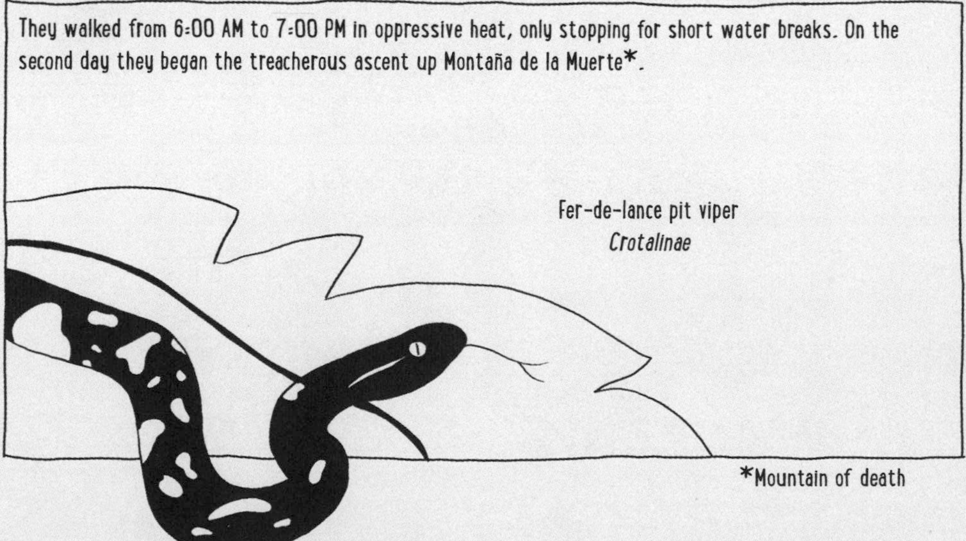

*Mountain of death

WATCH OUT!
Chunga palm
(with poison prickles)
Astrocaryum standleyanum

Thank Allah, Moussa takes such good care of us.

Jaguar
Panthera onca

After crossing the Darien Gap, the group kept heading north, walking through Panama, Costa Rica, and Central America until five months later they arrived at a Mexican border town on the edge of Texas.

In the first nine months of 2019, 80% of migrants treated by Medecins Sans Frontieres, an independent humanitarian organization, said they'd been victims of violence.

Moussa left Fanta at a church-run migrant shelter and disappeared. Fanta, who had picked up Spanish during her northward walk, was able to communicate with the staff there.

The shelter was in walking distance of the border.

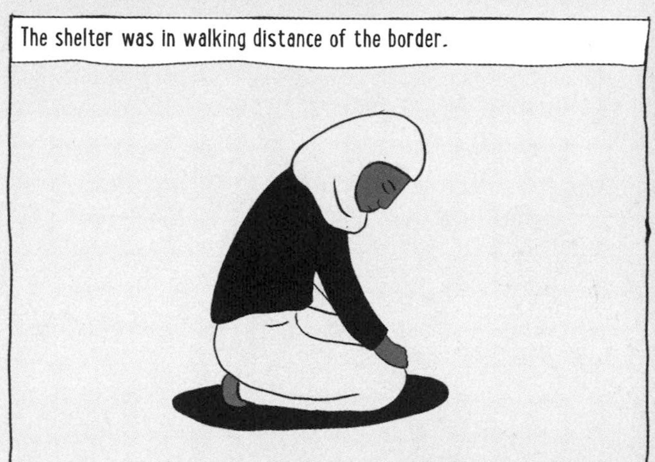

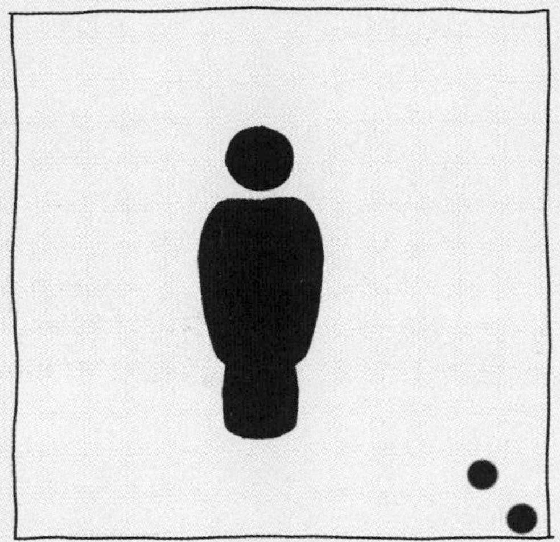

When a child goes to Immigration and Customs Enforcement (ICE) at the border on their own, ICE takes the Unaccompanied Refugee Minors (URM) into custody.

URM are placed in shelters (a network of state-licensed providers) until released to a US government-approved sponsor: family, friend, or foster care.

Sometimes, home studies are conducted to ensure a child's safety before being released. Follow-up services are provided for at-risk youth.

The cases slowly travel their way through the court system. The majority of children do not have legal representation.

Fanta was flown to a shelter for children in Chicago.

At the shelter she was assigned a team of case workers to help her. She became especially close to Ruby, her social worker, finally finding someone she could trust and confide in.

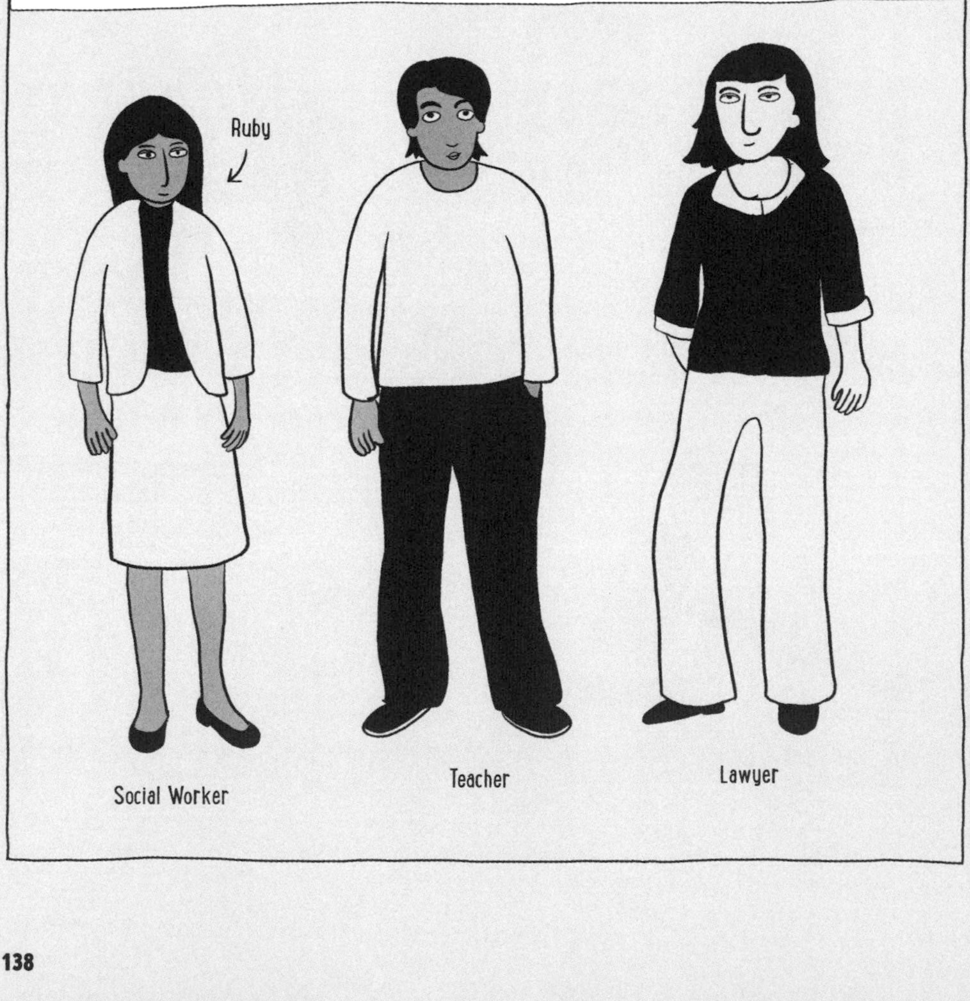

Ruby

Social Worker

Teacher

Lawyer

At the shelter she shared a room.
And this is your bed.

Fanta spoke French and Maninka, the language of her people, the Mandinke. It was the only language her mother spoke.
she ca go
I hope I learn English as quickly as I got Spanish.

To speak with her mom she faced a hurdle.
An interpreter must be in the room with you when you speak with your mom. We're having trouble finding someone who understands Maninka.

It took a month, but finally.
Fanta!!!!
Shelter phone. ↗ Fanta spoke in front of a social worker.

Oumar!
Mama!
Mariame!

Later in her room Fanta felt the weight of hearing her family's voices.
I miss my mother and children so much it hurts.

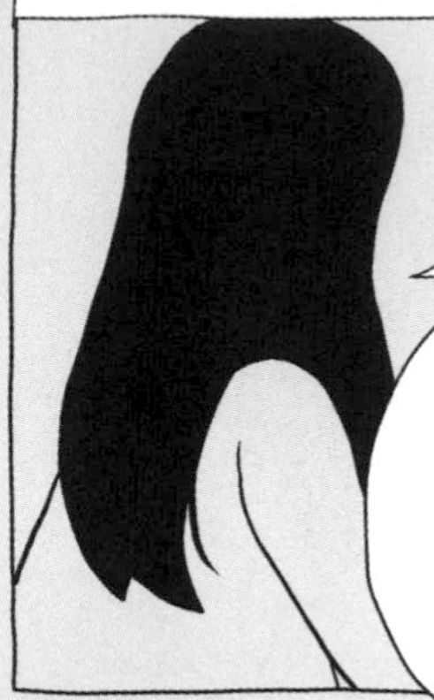
Fanta felt seen and safe with Ruby. She focused on learning English and telling Ruby her dreams. After two months her world changed again.
We have a foster home for you near New York City.
We'd prefer to place you in a Muslim home, but there is a wonderful foster mom who will provide good support for you now and you can leave the shelter.

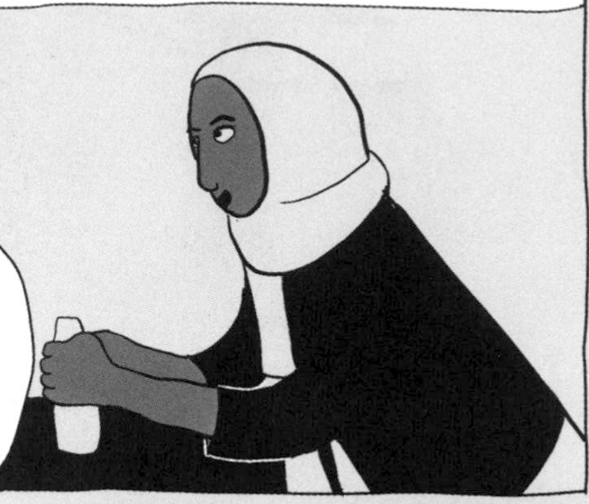

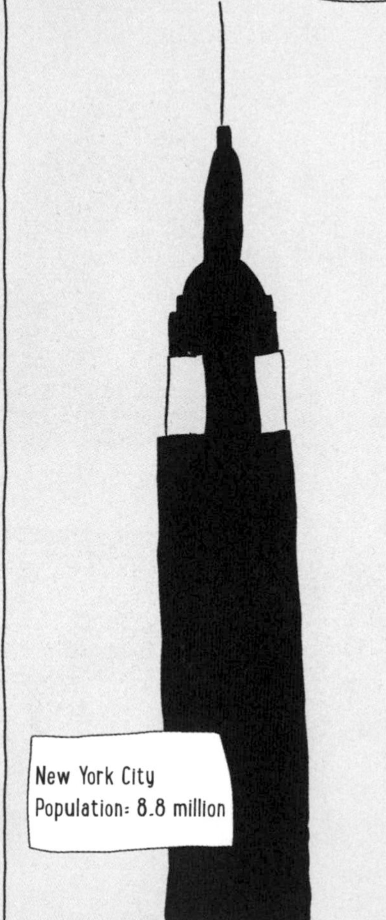
New York City
Population: 8.8 million

Thank you, Ruby.

Yonkers, NY
Population: 201 thousand

Welcome!
This is your room.
Feel free to come into the living room whenever you want.
Maybe the nightmares'll stop now that I'm in a real home.
You have a beautiful home.
And last but not least, our kitchen! Doesn't that smell good?
What's that smell? It hurts my nose.

Fanta was safe, but life was a constant adjustment. New language, new culture, new foods, and living in a non-Muslim home. Her foster mom had two other Spanish-speaking unaccompanied minors in the house. But Fanta felt there was little connection. None of them were parents. They hadn't left children behind.

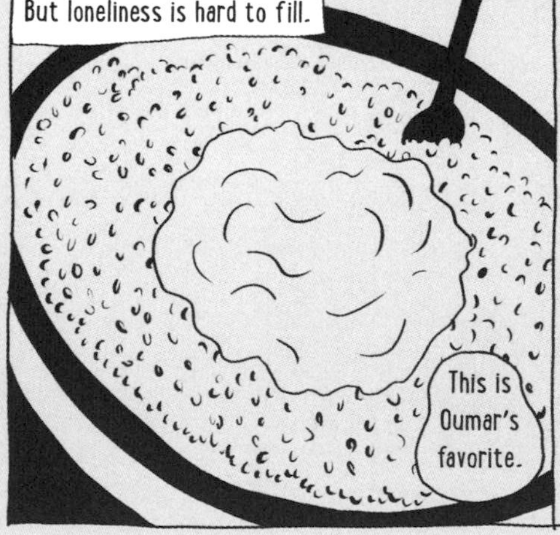

The real trouble was the phone.
You're allowed to make two calls a week from this phone.
Calls from your mother need to be between 7:00 AM and 10:00 PM.

Her mother's limited access to phone service plus the time difference meant she often called late at night.
ring, ring

FANTA!!

Your mother's alway calling when everyone is sleeping!
Tell her to stop.
Mama, she doesn't want me talking now. Cover Mariame and Oumar with hugs and kisses. I miss them so much my body aches.

Eventually the loneliness in the house and lack of cultural understanding were too much.
Things are not good here.

When another long-term option became available, Fanta moved to a new home in the Bronx.
Welcome!

If anything upsets or bothers you, let me know. It's just the two of us so we can sort it all out.
Thank you, I'm OK now.

Enrolled at an international public school, Fanta's dream of education was being realized.
Students in her ESL class

Fanta's days had changed, but not her nights.
STOOOOPPPPPPP!!

Fanta's foster mother was told about her PTSD and general history.
She cares!
Not again, this girl is exhausting me.
And then she woke me up at 2:30 AM! The third time this week.
I mean, if that's not crying for attention, I don't know what is.
I shouldn't listen by the door to her call, but I heard my name.
She says one thing and feels another. She's like my husband, good at hiding that the inside is rotten.
Allah will see me through.
Enough for me is Allah. There is no God but He.
In Him I have placed my trust, and He is the Lord of the Great Throne. (Quran 9:129)

Fanta's faith and inner strength sustained her while her lawyers worked to get her into a program that supported her education and her transition into a new community while also providing mental health and medical services as her case slowly went through the court system.

A few months after the incident at her second foster home, Fanta, with the help of her pro bono legal team, was accepted into the the Unaccompanied Refugee Minor program. The URM program provides culturally and linguistically appropriate foster care, educational support, and case management.

Fanta is currently living in a small city in the US. She is finishing high school, and the program she is in will help set her up for college. She still wants to be a doctor. Her dream is to help deliver babies.

She is focused on getting her children and mother into the United States as their sponsor. She is on track to receive her green card.

Author's Note

When I began research for what would become *Unaccompanied,* I started by interviewing lawyers from the Safe Passage Project who represent unaccompanied minors, and talking to them about their clients' common motivations for seeking asylum. There were two main reasons I spoke with lawyers instead of the minors themselves. First, when speaking directly to the teens there is always the possibility of reporting that could hurt a person's case, and second, to avoid retraumatization. One exception was "Fanta," who wanted her specific story to be told. Fanta and I corresponded through her lawyer to stay as close to her story as possible while making enough changes to protect her true identity. It took me a while to work through my interviews with the lawyers. I listened to them over and over again, paying close attention to specific experiences and details.

However, I soon realized that while the lawyers could speak in-depth about the most pertinent events that occurred, they had less information about their clients' day-to-day lives. Those details are not generally relevant for court cases. So, I began interviewing people with first- and secondhand knowledge of life before, during, and after the journey to discover the bigger picture around an individual's momentous choice to walk to the US. Then I wrote the first drafts of each chapter. My scripts started with words, more like a play.

I met with people who had similar lived experiences to the characters and they reviewed the information in every panel. I asked questions ranging from "Does this interaction feel authentic?" to "Are the items depicted on the shelves accurate?" This practice was integral. It was a constant learning process. As a documenter, I needed to hold myself accountable to these stories. I had to consider how my own point of view might influence these pages.

Nobody makes a book alone. *Unaccompanied* was the result of global collaboration among many people, but there is always more that can be added to the conversation. I have aimed to create a living document at www.traced.com/unaccompanied, where, working together, we can continue to list resources and expand upon our shared knowledge. This book is just one point of inquiry, not an answer.

Acknowledgments

A book like this can only come into existence with the partnership of people around the globe whose various areas of expertise and lived experiences helped support and respect the events depicted in these chapters.

These people are:
Cindy Abramson - JoJo Annobil - Dr. Yianella Blanco - Dr. Kimberly Joyce-Bernard - Mike Cavello – Jazmin Karolina Chavez - Ken Grobe - Sara Feldman LCSW - Marianela Fernandez - Ariana Mangual Figueroa - "Fanta" - Ana Joya - Elizabeth G. Kennedy - Aicha M. Keita -Jules Kramer - Isela Larreinaga - Stephanie Lopez – Mark Lane - Rich Leimsider - Adam Levy - Salvador Mendoza - Claude Meyers - Monica Trigos Padilla - Archi Pyati - Aisha Redux - Petronilla Rosa - Sam Roberts - John Shabliski - Saran Sidimi - Sharleen Smith - Ada Trillo - Kaavya Viswathan - Elizabeth Wood

Thank you to Catholic Charities, The Door, Jewish Family Service of San Diego, Minority Humanitarian Fund, Immigrant Justice Corp, Safe Passage Project, and School the World in Guatemala and Honduras.

Thank you to all the incredibly dedicated people who champion the human rights of children and teenagers around the world, including those who volunteer and work at the many shelters that sit at the Mexican/US border supporting refugees, migrants, and asylum seekers.

Thank you to Jisu Kim for your wise guidance and insightful edits.

Thank you to Emmanuel Guerisoli for your careful fact-checking and thought-provoking comments.

Liz Frances and the Street Noise team, thank you for your unwavering vision and support.

Janna Morishima, I'm grateful for your encouragement, advice, and guidance. Charlotte Sheedy, thank you for your belief in me over all these years.

Thank you, readers, for making space and time in your lives to think about this book.

Borderless love to my husband, Lakshman, and our children. You're everything to me.

Notes

Vilma

• Page 13, panel 2: According to the US Department of Labor, Child Labor Reports, Guatemala, 2020, in 2019 9% of children aged 7 to 14 were forced to work, most of this was in agriculture. See https://tinyurl.com/mhhke4dy

• Page 15, panel 1: "No more school." Compulsory education in Guatemala lasts 16 years from 4 to 15 years old. Enrollment rate for pre-primary education (4yo to 6yo) is around 48%, 92% for primary education (6yo to 13yo), and 47% for secondary education (13yo to 17yo). Source: UNESCO; see https://tinyurl.com/57c234d8

• Page 19, panel 4: Guatemalan law favors men in most matters. Source: Landa Ugarte, Ana; Salazar, Elizabeth; Quintana, Magali; Herrera, Molina Raul. USAID/Guatemala Gender Analysis Report. Prepared by Banyan Global, 2018. See https://tinyurl.com/bde22s22

Rosa

• Page 67, single panel: More info about the Unaccompanied Refugee Minors Program is available at https://tinyurl.com/3s62bztk. On migrants dying at the US border, see Mica Rosenberg, Kristina Cooke and Daniel Trotta, "The Border's Toll," Reuters, July 25, 2022; see https://tinyurl.com/bdxhfhdp

• Page 68, panel 1: On sponsors and the placement of refugee minors, see https://tinyurl.com/3dnssrdv

• Page 71, panel 2: On deportation proceedings, see https://www.usa.gov/deportation; on burden to prove need to stay, see https://tinyurl.com/2s4xe979.

• Page 74, panel 5: On ORR covering the minors' medical bills while in system, see https://tinyurl.com/mvvwtdye

Ricardo & Karen

• Page 86, panels 1 & 2: Ana Arana, "How the Street Gangs Took Central America," Foreign Affairs, May/June 2005; see https://tinyurl.com/3auw56ew

• Page 86, panel 5: Rosarlin Hernández, "Living in Fear: Children Displaced by Gang Extortion in El Salvador," UNICEF, August 2018; see https://tinyurl.com/52pj63px

• Page 88, panel 1: There are about 60,000 gang members across El Salvador, according to government estimates. Source: Human Rights Watch, El Salvador; see https://tinyurl.com/2ad6yfrb

• Page 96, panel 1: Tijuana is the busiest crossing point between Mexico and US. Source: https://tinyurl.com/52rx4mud

• Page 98, panel 1: Coyote smugglers charge up to $10,000. Source: https://openborders.info/human-smuggling-fees/

• Page 103, panel 1: At least 8,000 migrants have died trying to cross the US-Mexico border since 1998. Source: U.S. Border Patrol, 2021; see https://tinyurl.com/56vu58un
• Page 104, panel 5: Williams, S.C. & O'Meara, M. (2021), Services for Unaccompanied Refugee Minors: Select Findings from a Descriptive Study, OPRE Report #2021-81, Washington, DC: Office of Planning, Research, and Evaluation, Administration for Children and Families, U.S. Department of Health and Human Services; see https://tinyurl.com/yc6vchta
• Page 106, panel 6: Up to 71% of asylum cases are denied. Source: TRAC Immigration; see https://tinyurl.com/4hnpsujy
• Page 109, final panel: Current wait times for cases in the asylum backlog now average 1,621 days. This translates into 54 months or nearly four and a half years. Source: TRAC Immigration; see https://tinyurl.com/3xvtc3xh

Fanta

• Page 112, panel 3: 85% of Guinea's population is Muslim, and most of them follow Sunni traditions. Source: US Department of State, International Religious Freedom Report, 2018; see: https://tinyurl.com/pv43j35b
• Page 113, panel 2: According to Muslim law, nikah is a contract for the purpose of legalization of intercourse, procreation of children, and regulation of social life in the interest of society by creating the rights and duties between the parties themselves and between each of them and the children born from the union. Source: LL. B Mania, Marriage in Shia & Sunni law; see: https://tinyurl.com/4awhtcfn. Walima is a traditional marriage feast to publicize the union between two people. See https://tinyurl.com/mr4xr7hf
• Page 114, panel 2: 47% of girls in Guinea are married before their 18th birthday and 17% are married before the age of 15. Source: Institut National de la Statistique et ICF, Enquête Démographique et de Santé en Guinée 2018; see https://tinyurl.com/3279vr44. Child marriage is legally prohibited in Guinea. Source: Gender Index, Guinea Report; see https://tinyurl.com/mryzcchc
• Page 117, panel 5: 97% of women and girls have been subject to some form of FGM. Source: United Nation Populations Fund; see https://www.unfpa.org/data/fgm/GN. The FGM definition is from The World Health Organization (WHO) https://tinyurl.com/4kt4mw9e
• Page 122, panel 4: Domestic violence is not a crime in Guinea; therefore, police do not investigate such matters and refer to them as family issues. 7 of 10 women are subject to domestic violence in the country. Source: Immigration and Refugee Board of Canada, "Guinea: Domestic violence, including legislation, protection provided to victims and support services," October 2015; see https://tinyurl.com/5n76h8kn
• Page 132: For info on the Darien Gap and migrants, see Diana Roy, "Crossing the Darien Gap: Migrants Face Death on the Journey to the U.S.," Council on

Foreign Relations, June 22, 2022; see https://tinyurl.com/2dkr8kds. 134,000 migrants crossed the Darien Gap in 2021, 30,000 of them children; source: Lizabelt Avila & Maureen Meyer; "Beyond the U.S.-Mexico Border: Migration Trends in the Americas, Explained," WOLA, May 26, 2022; available at https://tinyurl.com/426rmzem. Migrants face human traffickers and guerrillas.Source: UNICEF, October 2021; see https://tinyurl.com/2krf2wn4

• Page 135, panel 5: Approximately 80% of the migrants treated by MSF teams in Nuevo Laredo (on the Mexico-US border) during the first nine months of 2019 reported having suffered at least one violent incident. Another 43.7% of patients said they had been victims of violence during the seven days prior to the consultation. Source: MSF, January 2020; see https://tinyurl.com/58tv7z5u

Glossary

asylee: A person who seeks protection in another country due to justifiable fears of persecution based on race, religion, nationality, political belief, or membership in a specific social group. The application process occurs in the desired country or at a port of entry to the desired country. For more see https://tinyurl.com/yc3kbj7k

Customs and Border Protection (CBP): The largest branch of the Department of Homeland Security. And according to the CBP website, the CBP "is charged with keeping terrorists and their weapons out of the U.S. while facilitating lawful international travel and trade." This includes ensuring that customs, immigration, trade, and agriculture at the U.S. border are secure. For more see https://www.cbp.gov/about

coyote: Someone who smuggles people across the Mexico–United States border for money. *Coyote* is a Mexican Spanish word that historically describes a type of North American wild dog.

Department of Homeland Security (DHS): According to the DHS website it is "the U.S. federal executive department responsible for public security. Its mission is to protect America from terrorism, ensure border security, regulate immigration and customs, and manage cyber security and disaster prevention." For more see https://www.dhs.gov/about-dhs

Department of Health and Human Services (HHS): According to the HHS website, "HHS must provide care for each unaccompanied child, defined as a child who has no lawful immigration status in the United States; has not attained 18 years of age; and, with respect to whom, there is no parent or legal guardian in the United States, or no parent or legal guardian in the United States available to provide care and physical custody." For more see https://tinyurl.com/mrxencn

Flores settlement agreement: According to the National Immigration Forum, "the Flores agreement (1997) guarantees a number of rights to detained migrant children, including the right to be held in the least restrictive setting appropriate while in detention and the right to be released from government custody without delay to parents, family members, or appropriate guardians." For more see https://tinyurl.com/bdfa3fsz

human smuggling: The voluntary, usually paid illegal transportation of people over borders.

human trafficking: The involuntary moving and selling of people. Every day, all over the world, human beings are deceived, exploited, and trafficked most often for forced labor, domestic slavery, sexual exploitation, involuntary organ removal, and child begging.

immigrant: A person who lives permanently in a different country from the one they were born in.

Immigration and Nationality Act, Section 292: Asylum seekers have the right to legal counsel (but not a right to government-funded legal counsel). That is why free legal representation is so important for unaccompanied minors (and all asylum seekers). See https://tinyurl.com/3tmesf7b

Immigration and Customs Enforcement (ICE): As described on the ICE website, "ICE is a division of Homeland Security tasked with protecting America from the cross-border crime and illegal immigration that threaten national security and public safety." See https://www.ice.gov/mission

migrant: The International Center for Migration defines a migrant as "a person who moves away from his or her place of usual residence, whether within a country or across an international border, temporarily or permanently, and for a variety of reasons." See https://www.iom.int/who-migrant-0

Northern Triangle Countries (NTC): The countries of Honduras, El Salvador, and Guatemala are referred to as the Northern Triangle Countries. They are neighboring Central American countries each with their own histories, cultures, and dialects but which share similar challenges.

Office of Refugee Resettlement (ORR): According to the ORR website, they attempt to "place an unaccompanied child in the least restrictive setting that is in the best interests of the child, taking into consideration danger to self, danger to the community, and risk of flight. ORR takes into consideration the unique nature of each child's situation and incorporates child welfare principles when making placement, clinical, case management, and release decisions that are in the best interest of the child. ORR provides new populations with the opportunity to achieve their full potential in the United States." See https://tinyurl.com/2p8naywh

refugee: According to the United Nations Refugee Agency, "refugees are people who have fled war, violence, conflict, or persecution and have crossed an international border to find safety in another country. Refugees are defined and protected in international law. The 1951 Refugee Convention is a key legal document and defines a refugee as 'someone who is unable or unwilling to return to their country of origin owing to a well-founded fear of being persecuted for reasons of race, religion, nationality, membership of a particular social group, or political opinion.' " See https://tinyurl.com/yckuf5rc

Unaccompanied Alien Child Protection Act of 2005 (UACPA): Sought to address the "holes in our immigration system" around asylum-seeking minors coming to the United States on their own. See https://tinyurl.com/unbwpnhw

unaccompanied minor: The United Nations defines an unaccompanied minor as a person under 18 who is "separated from both parents and is not being cared for by an adult who by law or custom has responsibility to do so." See https://www.unhcr.org/3d4f91cf4.pdf

Unaccompanied Refugee Minor (URM): The ORR defines a URM as a child under 18 with "no lawful immigration status in the United States [and] no parent or legal guardian in the United States [who] is available to provide care and physical custody." See https://tinyurl.com/59tbfd4v

Further Reading

CENTRAL AMERICA BY COUNTRY

El Salvador (History)

Almeida, Paul D. *Waves of Protest: Popular Struggle in El Salvador, 1925-2005.* University of Minnesota Press, 2008.

El Salvador (Literature, Poetry, Testimonials)

Pineda, Janel. *Lineage of Rain.* Haymarket Books, 2021.

Zamora, Javier. *Unaccompanied.* Copper Canyon Press, 2017.

Guatemala (History)

Grandin, Greg, et al. *The Guatemala Reader: History, Culture, Politics.* Duke University Press, 2011.

Guatemala (Literature, Poetry, Testimonials)

Ak'abal, Humberto. *Aquí era el paraíso: Selección de poemas de Humberto Ak'abal.* Groundwood Books / House of Anansi Press, 2021.

Belize (History)

Leslie, Robert, and Rachel Heusner. *A History of Belize: Nation in the Making.* Cubola Productions, 2013.

Belize (Literature, Poetry, Testimonials)

Edgell, Zee. *Beka Lamb.* Heinemann, 1983.

Honduras (History)

Cardoza, Melissa. *13 Colors of the Honduran Resistance.* Translated by Matt Ginsberg-Jaeckle, El BeiSMan Press, 2016.

Honduras (Literature, Poetry, Testimonials)

Nazario, Sonia. *Enrique's Journey.* Random House Trade Paperbacks, 2014.

Nicaragua (History)

Kinzer, Stephen. *Blood of Brothers, Life and War in Nicaragua.* Harvard University Press, 2007.

Nicaragua (Literature, Poetry, Testimonials)

Belli, Gioconda, and Kristina Cordero. *The Country under My Skin: A Memoir of Love and War.* Anchor Books, 2003.

Costa Rica (History)

Palmer, Steven, and Iván Molina. *The Costa Rica Reader: History, Culture, Politics.* Duke University Press, 2004.

BOOKS ABOUT CENTRAL AMERICA FOCUSED ON THE REGION AS A WHOLE

Galeano, Eduardo. *Open Veins of Latin America. Five Centuries of the Pillage of a Continent.* Translated by Cedric Belfrage, Monthly Review Press, 1973.

LaFeber, Walter. *Inevitable Revolutions: The United States in Central America.* W.W. Norton, 1993.

González Juan. *Harvest of Empire: A History of Latinos in America.* Penguin Books, 2022.

Hernández Linares, Leticia, et al. *The Wandering Song: Central American Writing in the United States.* Tía Chucha Press, 2020.

Booth, John A., et al. *Understanding Central America: Global Forces, Rebellion, and Change.* Westview Press, 2006.

Rodríguez, Ana Patricia. *Dividing the Isthmus: Central American Transnational Histories, Literatures, and Cultures.* University of Texas Press, 2009.

Alvarez, Julia, et al. *Resistencia: Poems of Protest and Revolution.* Tin House, 2020.

Villalobos, Juan Pablo. *The Other Side: Stories of Central American Teen Refugees Who Dream of Crossing the Border.* Square Fish, 2022.

Levi, Enrique Jaramillo, et al. *Contemporary Short Stories from Central America.* University of Texas Press, 1994.

Voces Sin Fronteras: Our Stories, Our Truth. Shout Mouse Press, 2018.

GUINEA, AFRICA

For a comprehensive take on post colonial Guinean history see Camara, Mohamed Saliou. *Political History of Guinea since World War Two.* Peter Lang, 2014.

For precolonial history see Davidson, Basil. *West Africa before the Colonial Era: A History to 1850.* Routledge, 2015.

For history on the French colonial rule see Klein, Martin. *Slavery and Colonial Rule in French West Africa.* Cambridge University Press, 1998.

For background on the spread of Islam into West Africa see Robinson, David. *Muslim Societies in African History.* Cambridge University Press, 2011.

For history and culture see Alvin, Emmanuel. *Guinea Conakry: African Art, Culture, Politics, Economy: Inside-out of Guinea and Africa.* Alvinston Publishing, 2016.

Study Guide Questions

Context

Each chapter includes a map of the region where the main storyteller and their family is from.

Why is understanding this geography important? How does the geographical context add to your understanding of their journeys? Of the challenges that come with migration?

What do you know about this country's languages, cultures, people, and history? How do you know this?

What are two questions that you have in regards to the social, cultural, political, and historical context of this country?

Books as Windows and Mirrors

Books can provide windows (perspectives/experiences different from your own) and mirrors (perspectives/experiences that remind you of yourself).

Can you identify specific windows and mirrors in the lived experiences of the speakers, characters, and content of the book?

Which individual story resonated with you the most? Why? Which individual story challenged you the most? Why? What idea resonates with you from one of the personal narratives and your own life experiences?

What did you learn while reading these stories? How could you apply this knowledge?

Compare your storyteller's identity groups (race, gender, ethnicity, sexual orientation, immigration status, ability, class, language, and/or religion, etc.) to your own identity groups. What identities are shared and what identities are not shared?

Social identity is a person's sense of who they are based on their group membership(s). Consider one storyteller's social identity. What labels do they use to describe their identity in different social groups? What labels do others or society assign to them? How does the storyteller deal with the disconnect between how they define themselves and how others may perceive them?

The narrative identity is the internal story that you tell yourself that connects memories from the past with the present and ideas about the future. What do you think each storyteller wants you, the reader, to understand about who they are through the story they tell? How do you know this?

Immigration

Central Americans and Africans are often depicted in the media and in Hollywood as deficient—marked by trauma, poverty, and violence. How do the stories in this book challenge those depictions? Where do you see instances of hope, joy, and strength?

All of the storytellers in this book had to go through the immigration process at one point in their journeys. What did you learn about this process? What surprised you?

Stories about immigration are often told about immigrants rather than by them. How do the storytellers demonstrate courage, agency, and power within themselves and their circumstances?

What are stereotypes that exist about immigration? Why do people form stereotypes? When are stereotypes harmful? What can people do to limit the stereotypes they have about immigrants from the countries that our storytellers are from?

What seem to be the root causes of one of the issues/problems addressed? What kinds of activities are currently taking place in the storytellers' communities and in your own community related to this issue/problem?

What impacts the way you view the situation/experience of migration? In what ways have your own lived experiences shaped that view? And now, how has the personal narrative you read here impacted that view?

Complete the following sentence: Before I read this book, my views about immigration were ______________________________, but now I think ________________________________.

Opportunity

Family is an important theme across all of the stories in this book. In what ways are the storytellers motivated by their commitment to their families? How do their families provide support?

Each of the storytellers utilized resources (social and economic capital and political structures), strategy, and people to assist them with their migration journey. What contributed to their successful migration? What hindered their success? What follow-up is needed to address any challenges?

Potentially Sensitive and Upsetting Content

Physical and sexual abuse is discussed openly in these chapters (and in other narratives by Central American migrants). What responsibilities do we (as communities, schools, neighbors) have to support survivors? What resources should we have available?

The abusers in these stories were often men. Are there specific implicit and explicit messages that boys receive while growing up that can shape their beliefs about what it means to be a man, and that create a narrow idea of masculinity? How do men earn respect from their peers, family, and society from the perspective of the storyteller and from your own lived experiences?

By Dr. Kimberly Joyce-Bernard and Dr. Yianella Blanco